The Cow
in the
Parking
Lot

A Zen Approach
to Overcoming
Anger

Leonard Scheff and Susan Edmiston

WORKMAN PUBLISHING • NEW YORK

The parables on pages 70, 88, 113, 116, and 130 are reprinted
from *Zen Flesh, Zen Bones*, by Paul Reps and Ngoyen Sensak,
copyright © 1985 by permission of the publisher, Weatherhill.

Excerpts in chapter 10 from "Those Aren't Fighting Words, Dear," © August
2, 2009, *The New York Times*. All rights reserved. Used by permission and
protected by the copyright laws of the United States.

Excerpts on pages 179–183 and 184 from *Anger* by Thich Nhat Hanh,
copyright © 2001 by Thich Nhat Hanh. Used by permission of Riverhead
Books, an imprint of Penguin Group (USA) Inc.

Library of Congress Cataloging-in-Publication Data
Scheff, Leonard.
The cow in the parking lot : a zen approach to overcoming anger /
by Leonard Scheff and Susan Edmiston.
p. cm.
ISBN 978-0-7611-5815-8 (alk. paper)
1. Anger. 2. Anger—Prevention. I. Edmiston, Susan. II. Title.
BF575.A5S333 2010
294.3'444—dc22   2010006829

Workman Publishing Company, Inc.
225 Varick Street
New York, NY 10014-4381
www.workman.com

Printed in the United States of America
First printing June 2010

10 9 8 7 6 5 4 3 2 1

In memory of John Clayton Bilby,
friend and teacher

CONTENTS

You are at the grand opening of a new shopping mall on the edge of town. You've been driving around looking for a parking space for ten minutes. At last, right in front of you, a car pulls out of a spot. You hit your turn signal and wait as the car backs out. Suddenly, from the other direction, comes a Jeep that pulls into the space. Not only that, but when you honk, the driver gets out, smirks, and gives you the finger. Are you angry?

Now change the scene ever so slightly. Instead of a brash Jeep driver, a cow walks into the space from the other direction and settles down in the middle of it. When you honk, she looks up and moos but doesn't budge. Are you angry?

> —The Cow in the Parking Lot,
> A Contemporary Zen Parable

Introduction

Most people, if asked, would agree that we would be better off without anger. Yet anger seems to be a growth industry, which, unfortunately of late, has entered a new phase of destructiveness. Today, we live in a society marked by road rage, spousal abuse, professionally angry TV and radio commentators, teenagers who go on deadly rampages, and an "us versus them" mentality. We live in daily fear of super vandals who are willing to kill thousands to vent their anger.

The question is, why does anger not only persist but increase?

First, anger is a normal human emotion. Everyone gets angry. Someone once asked the Dalai Lama what he thought of people who study the teachings of Buddhism and then use that knowledge to make money. His response was temperate at first. But as he went on, he grew red in the face. Even though he is the human embodiment of patience and compassion, the Dalai Lama himself has admitted that he gets angry. The object of this book is not to eliminate anger but to place it and our expression of it in a different context.

The second reason for the persistence of anger is that there is no obvious alternative. This book will offer one based on Buddhist teachings, but it does not require any specific religious belief. Nor is it psychotherapy except as Gestalt therapist Fritz Perls once said, "Awareness is therapy *per se.*" A fair summary of this book is: You are hitting your hand with a hammer. If you stop, you will feel better.

We have been conditioned in many ways to use anger as a tool for obtaining our ends. Most people do not question this practice and are almost completely oblivious to its costs. My experience in teaching my workshop is that once people realize there is an alternative, their anger begins to dissipate.

The third reason for the persistence of anger is that it is addictive. There is a physical and emotional high that comes with feeling anger. The physical sensation is set off by the release of adrenaline with its resulting increase in blood pressure. This anger "high" becomes addictive much as smoking or drinking does. Like other addictions, anger has its price, which can include heart attack, stroke, and other health problems. I have heard people say, "I only feel really alive when I am angry." That is like saying, "I only feel really healthy when I am smoking." Both are examples of how wrong we can be when living in what Buddhism calls *maya*, the world of illusion created by our thoughts.

The conventional addictions, smoking and drinking, are difficult to give up in part because, if you are successful, you may feel like hell for weeks, months, or even years. Recovering alcoholics often say, "There isn't a waking hour that goes by, that I don't want to have a drink."

The good news about reducing or giving up anger is that from the very first time you choose not to be angry or not to act out your anger, you feel better. Once you've experienced the difference, you will not want to return to that habit.

Some people may argue that anger is necessary and serves useful purposes. True, when we become angry, it may be an indication that something is wrong with the way we are relating to others or to our environment. Anger can also galvanize us to act on something we believe is morally wrong. When you see someone abusing a child, a form of anger that may be called moral indignation arises. But if your remedy is pursued in hot-headedness, it may well worsen the situation. If you see a mother repeatedly slapping a child, you may want to interfere physically, perhaps even by hitting the mother. That may interrupt the abuse for the moment, but the mother may well add that provocation to her reasons for continuing to abuse the child at a later time.

On the other hand, if you look at the available options with a cooler head, you may find a way to intervene that does not heighten the conflict between mother and child. Sitting next to them in such a way that the mother is embarrassed to continue the abuse may provide a temporary solution, and may lead to a beneficial conversation without promoting further anger against the child.

To act out of moral indignation demands that we pause to consider the best options for putting the situation right. When we act solely out of anger, with little regard for consequences, we are not pursuing the greater good but are only assuaging our own emotional distress. And the result could make the situation worse rather than better. Certain disciplines, in particular the martial arts, teach that when you act out of anger you are more likely to lose.

Many people believe that they can't help acting on their angry feelings. They see no space between becoming angry and expressing that anger. They believe that they have no control over and no choice about the anger they feel. One of the lessons of this book is that we can consciously create a space between the rise of anger and the actions we take as a result.

When you apply the techniques offered here with ongoing success, you are more than likely to feel an increase in self-esteem. No longer does your anger control you—you control your anger. Unlike the self-esteem that comes from without ("You look good today"; "You did a good job"), this feeling is not dependent on others' perceptions.

It is quite possible—and even reasonable—that you may greet the foregoing ideas with skepticism. The notion that you can do without anger may seem contrary to your conditioning, as it did to mine when I attended the teachings of the Dalai Lama, in Tuscon, Arizona, in 1993.

There for the first time, I heard someone tell me that anger was destructive and that I could live without it. As a member of the notoriously contentious legal profession, I believed that anger was not only necessary and useful but also essential to my personality and sense of self. For various reasons, I was seated in the middle of the front row for all four days of the teachings. If I missed a session or fell asleep, I was sure His Holiness would notice. Even though I knew he wouldn't care, I didn't want to offend the people who had arranged for me to have the best seat in the house.

As it became clear that he was suggesting that my life would be better without anger, I became increasingly uncomfortable. I believed that anger was what protected me from a world that wanted a piece of me, that it gave me

control over the people around me. So there I was, forced
to pay attention to something that I did not agree with. I
thought to myself: This is a really nice man, but if he thinks
I'm going to give up anger, he's crazy. I still felt that way
when I left the four-day seminar.

The very next night I was driving home when someone
cut so closely in front of my car that I was forced to hit
the brake pedal. I honked the horn. The driver turned his
head just long enough to scream an obscenity at me. I felt
like ramming his car or at least shouting back in return.
But I stopped myself—it occurred to me that having spent
four miserable days at the teachings, perhaps I should try
to apply them. I asked myself what it was that made me
angry, and understood that it was that this total stranger had
disrespected me. I also recognized that his insult in itself was
harmless; I was the one who was giving it meaning. When I
realized that, I started laughing—at myself. Then I felt how
much better it was to be laughing instead of fulminating.

That was my first inkling of what the Dalai Lama
had been teaching, and from then on I began a process
of conscientiously studying and experimenting with his
teachings. As I did so, I found my life improving. The price of
anger and the lack of benefits became clearer. My wife and I,
who had been going through a rough patch in our marriage,
reversed direction and have had an improved relationship

ever since. My practice as a litigation and transaction lawyer became less stressful and, surprisingly, more successful.

When I was a chronically angry attorney, I would start a conversation with the opposing lawyer with a polite form of "What the hell does your client think she's doing?" I would never concede that my client could conceivably be at fault. Needless to say, I didn't settle many cases. Now I start the conversation with something like, "I am not sure I understand what is going on here. Would you explain your client's position?" Or I might offer or concede that my client failed to do something, like leaving out an important element in a sales contract. The result is that there is less posturing on both sides and cases get settled.

I found myself happier than I had ever been or thought I could be. Wanting to share my experience with others, I developed a three-hour workshop called "Transforming Anger," in which I tried to make some of the Dalai Lama's teachings accessible to those who had no acquaintance with Buddhism. I added some exercises and ideas from other disciplines that I thought would be helpful. When someone suggested that I write a book based on the workshop, I realized that I could reach a wider audience and perhaps in some small way even improve the world we live in.

I took the book *The Zen of Running* by Fred Rohe as my model because of its simplicity. Its two basic ideas were that if you want to run, start out slowly and do it in a way that makes it enjoyable. Don't try to run five miles on the first day. You may run the five miles but you probably won't become a runner because unconsciously or consciously you don't want to do anything that painful. Also, find a place and time to run that makes it easy for you. Because, if you don't enjoy it, you're not going to do it for very long.

I have tried to observe these principles in approaching the subject of anger, that is, to keep each step in the process as simple as possible and build on the positive results that make the process rewarding. In the second chapter the reader is advised to start by looking at small irritations that cause his or her anger and to put off dealing with more profound sources of pain. To do otherwise would be like running five miles the first day.

Readers will not be asked to examine difficult parts of their lives. No psychological analysis is required. There's no need to open the dark recesses of the unconscious to learn what this book has to teach. As anger is overcome and you understand better what irritates you about small things, you become more capable of delving into larger issues.

The book invites you to experiment with your life. It is interactive, with writing exercises that ask you to examine incidents in your life and perhaps the motives behind them. There are no right or wrong answers. It is

the willingness to observe and examine oneself that drives
the process.

Finally, this book is meant to challenge your beliefs
about anger and cast doubt on the value of using it as a way
of getting what you want. As those beliefs slowly erode,
your perspective will change and you will never be able to
think of anger, or be angry, in the same way again. The very
first time you make a choice not to be angry, you will find
yourself on a more pleasurable path.

The transformation that began for me after hearing
the Dalai Lama is available to everyone. I hope that by
reading this book and practicing its teachings in your
life, you will find the contentment that comes from the
absence of anger, and that its companion emotions of
jealously, resentment, and insecurity will also be reduced.
If you are comfortable with and use the concepts offered
here, I believe that profound changes in your life and your
relationships will follow.

—Leonard Scheff

CHAPTER 1

A New Approach to Dealing with Anger

You are at the opening of a new shopping center on the edge of town. Since all the stores are having Grand Opening sales and giveaways, half the town is there. You have been looking for a parking space for ten minutes. At last, right in front of you, back-up lights come on. You hit your turn signal and wait as the car backs out in front of you. From the other direction comes a Jeep that pulls into the space. Not only that, but when you honk, the driver gets out, smirks, and gives you the finger. Are you angry? You bet you are! What would you like to do at this point?

- Ram his car

- Let the air out of his tires

- Key his car

- Take out a lipstick and write "jerk" on his windshield

Doubtless, we've all fantasized—at least—about one or all of these options. Entire movies have been built around the unexpected and untoward results, including murder, of such petty fits of revenge. You may imagine that expressing your anger—ramming the offending car, and so on—may help it to go away. But let's look at the specific costs of these various options.

- Ramming his car will likely damage yours, and if a security guard sees you there may be a criminal charge. At the very least, the security guard will take your license number and put it under the Jeep's windshield wipers for the owner to find. He will not care one bit that you think you had good cause.

- Letting the air out of the culprit's tires takes a lot of nerve. Can you imagine the tension you would be under wondering, as the air slowly seeped out, what would happen if the driver came back to the car for something he forgot? As in the first scenario, the guard who happened by would not see this as a prank.

• The lipstick option is more benign, but even a fast scrawl takes time, and you'd certainly ruin the lipstick. Again, it is vandalism and if a security guard sees you, well as they say in Spanish, *"No vale la pena."* ("It's not worth it.")

But the main cost may be that you continue to carry that anger around with you for days, or longer, to be reactivated each time you search for a parking place.

How Revenge Backfires

As an exercise, close your eyes for a moment and imagine that the parking offense has just happened to you. Feel the anger rise. Then imagine that you take revenge with any of the above remedies or one of your own choosing.

Now ask yourself if you are any less angry. If your answer is that your anger has gone away, then add to the fantasy the fact that you have been compelled by this lout to commit a violent and possibly criminal act.

Is your anger really gone? Now you are fearful that you may run into the driver or that you will be apprehended for committing a crime.

✦ *Exercise* WRITE A NOTE

Pretend that you have been the victim of this outrage.
Instead of committing a criminal act, write a note to the Jeep
driver in the space below. Keep it short but tell him what you
would say to him if you could do so without fear of reprisal.

_____

_____

_____

_____

_____

_____

_____

Now imagine a different scenario. Same scene, back-up
lights, car pulls out in front of you. However, instead
of our smirking young man, a cow walks into the space from
the other direction and settles down right in the middle of
it. Remember this is on the outskirts of town. It so happens
that the cow has spent every afternoon in that spot for years.
When you honk, she looks up and moos but doesn't budge.
Are you angry?

The answer for almost everyone is, "No, I'm not angry; I'm amused." So the question is, "What is the difference?"

This book hopes to convince you that there is no difference.

Whether it was the guy in the Jeep or the cow, the outcome is exactly the same: You need to find another parking spot. The only thing that changes is your *reaction* to the outcome. In other words, no one *causes* us to be angry. Anger is not inevitable. Anger begins and ends with ourselves.

But, some people argue, there is a difference because the guy intended his actions and the cow didn't. We'll look at that more closely later, but for now, let's accept that as true. Does this justify your anger and your desire to express it?

What Are the Benefits of Anger?

Many of us believe that there are benefits to acting out anger. One notion is that to express it—no matter how inappropriately—is preferable to holding it in, that suppressing your anger may even lead to disease. But in the exercise above, where you imagined that this happened to you, you probably became aware that acting out your anger, if anything, augments it. The act of revenge is more likely to increase your anger than reduce it. So cross that possible benefit off your list.

Some of us justify expressing anger as a "moral duty to reform the offender" or at least let him know our opinion of his actions. Let's say that we have written "jerk" on his windshield. What will his reaction be when he arrives back at his car after several hours of shopping. There are two possibilities:

He will look at his windshield and say: "My gosh! I have sinned. I have committed an offense against another human. I am grateful someone has taken the time to bring my unacceptable conduct to my attention. I will never steal someone's parking space again."

Or, he will look at his windshield and say: "You SOB! Look what that *&%#%& has done to my windshield! Why do these things happen to me? If only I could find out who did it, I'd show him a thing or two."

Although theoretically there may be two possibilities, we know that only the second one is likely. The offender has already identified himself as an angry person by his response to your honk. No doubt, he has rationalized his conduct to his satisfaction. "I saw the place first," "I was in a hurry and needed it more," and so on. His high level of anger may indicate that he already views himself, probably accurately, as unloved and unappreciated. This latest incident is just one more example of how the world treats him unfairly. You may believe there's such a thing as a social contract that requires that we treat one another with decency. Unfortunately, many people act on this only when it serves their self-interest. When they are dishing it out, their motto becomes, "It's a tough world out there, and survival is to the swift."

So now our Jeep owner drives off, peering around the word "jerk" on his windshield and growing angrier and angrier with perhaps a dollop of shame added to the poisonous brew. His shopping high has worn off, and by the time he gets home, he has a full head of steam. Does it end there? Of course, it doesn't. That anger will be taken out on the next convenient victim.

So rather than reforming him, you have given him additional impetus to express his already uncontrollable anger. Someone downstream will suffer. It may be his wife, his children, or another stranger who happens to be in his way. Once you think it through, it is reasonably clear that acting out your anger has not only harmed him but also those who must deal with him. So before deciding to reform someone without his cooperation, ask yourself if you want to be responsible for his entirely predictable response to your efforts.

There is a third reason some people use to rationalize expressing their anger: If I don't, I will feel powerless, i.e., victimized. However, I hope to show that true power comes when we control our anger and not when we allow it to control us.

The Question of Intention

Now let's look at the assumption that the brash young man, unlike the cow, intended the effects his action had on you. Most likely, he is oblivious to the feelings of people around him. How many times have you said or done something that offended someone else and been surprised at the response?

Most of the time, when people act offensively, their behavior is not aimed at us. Even if there is no doubt the offender is talking to you, or interacting with you, what he says most likely has nothing to do with who you are or what you have done. It's not personal; he doesn't know you. You just happen to be a stage prop in an internal drama taking place in his mind.

The mental scenarios most of us create are a mixture of our view of the world, our view of ourselves, our early conditioning, and habitual ways of responding. They often have little to do with the reality of the present situation. So when our conditioning calls for us to react with outrage to something offensive, we do so, even if our reaction is totally counterproductive. We follow our own script. When it doesn't produce the expected results and even makes us miserable, we still continue to follow our script, but now with an increased sense of outrage and martyrdom.

So if we reconsider the Jeep driver's behavior, we see that the line between intentional and unintentional is not as clear as we would like to think. We may believe that we know what another person is thinking, but most often our efforts at "mind reading" are projections of our own inner, self-centered concerns.

◆

I began with the parable of "The Cow in the Parking Lot" to illustrate some aspects of this book's approach to anger. Anger is often an immediate but irrational reaction based on a notion we have in our heads. What we feel is based to a great degree on what we think. Our fantasized imagining of the Jeep driver's intentions affects how we view "reality" and therefore our reaction to it. In this case, we believe that the Jeep driver has intended to offend, while we know that the cow bears us no grudges; she's just behaving like a cow. It's a simple example of how we create our reality—and therefore our anger—with our minds. As the Buddha says,

We are what we think.
All that we are arises with our thoughts.
With our thoughts we make the world.

Much of what's in our heads is the result of our early conditioning. These beliefs are often referred to in Western psychology as "baggage." For example, we are conditioned to believe that certain things will make us happy, and when we do not get them we are angry. We are conditioned to believe that our honor is at stake if someone "disses" us. We are conditioned to think that achieving a certain goal in the future, rather than living in the present, will make us happy. And we are conditioned to believe that anger is a useful tool in getting what we want.

Buddhism is not a religion in the sense of worshipping a god or embracing a system of beliefs, but its techniques offer a method for overcoming our conditioning. The essential tool of this method is the practice of awareness. The word *buddha*, itself, comes from the Sanskrit root meaning "awake," or "aware." Buddhism's central vow is, "I take refuge in buddha," which refers not to taking refuge in a god or iconic being but in the quality of "awareness" that such beings have in common.

This may seem simple—and in a sense it is. But it involves a radical change in how we view our minds, our intellects. What Buddhism means by being awake or aware is being present in each moment and experiencing it directly without being limited by all the beliefs, concepts, and assumptions that many of us confuse with knowledge. The Buddha illustrates this with a simple example: "A man shudders with horror when he steps upon a serpent, but laughs when he looks down and sees that it is only a rope." The idea or concept of a snake, or serpent, is a construction created by the mind and is a useful one for navigating a jungle or a forest. But to one who is awake or aware, there is only a brown curving thing lying on the ground. To see, or be aware of, what is actually before one's eyes requires a kind of attention that in Buddhism is called "mindfulness."

If we can be fully present in the moment and observe what we are experiencing directly without allowing the intervention of previous interpretations or beliefs, this is awareness. Seeing the world in this way makes our lives more vivid and immediate, enables a flexibility of response in each moment, and creates the possibility of change.

One specific technique that Buddhism teaches for facilitating awareness is called "bare attention" or sometimes, "bare noting." We don't say "snake," we say "brown, round thing, curving on the ground." We observe without judging or interpreting. Of course, if the thing then begins to hiss or writhe, we say "snake" and act accordingly. But if we can acquire the habit of observing first with an open mind— "with naked awareness of what *is* before conceptual thought arises," as Buddhist writer Steve Hagen puts it—we can escape our habitual reactions. By this method, we can also observe ourselves, our moods, our prejudices, and our habits. Change comes, not by struggling to change or by fighting or disciplining oneself, but by becoming aware of what we are feeling and how we habitually act.

This book uses the ideas and techniques of Buddhism, but it does not ask you to accept a particular spiritual view. It requires only that you suspend for a moment any belief that anger is a useful, necessary tool or an essential part of your personality.

The Process

The process offered by the book is based on five working hypotheses. They are:

• **Anger is a destructive emotion.**

• **The first person damaged by your anger is you.**

• **When you act out of anger, you will act irrationally.**

• **You can, if you choose, reduce the amount of anger in your life.**

• **As you reduce anger in your life, you will be happier and more effective.**

You do not need to accept any of these as true; you need only to be open and willing to experiment with them. If you believe even one of them is useful and act on it in your daily life, this book will accomplish its purpose. Now let's take a look at some of these hypotheses.

First, the destructiveness of anger in our world is almost too obvious to require discussion. The notion that revenge is the proper remedy for anger fuels destruction for generations. Every day the classic clan feud between the Hatfields and the McCoys gets played out in large and small arenas. Among the global examples are the conflicts between Catholics and Protestants in Ireland, Israelis and Palestinians in the Middle East, and Hindus and Muslims in India.

At the other extreme, we constantly encounter expressions of anger that are as astounding in their silliness as they are potentially lethal in their effects. People have been murdered in disputes over parking spaces, and moments of intemperate rage can irrevocably damage precious relationships.

Second, anger is toxic to our bodies and health. A recent review of more than forty scientific studies has confirmed the strong association of anger and hostility with the onset of coronary heart disease in healthy people as well as a poor prognosis for those already suffering from it. When someone with risk factors for heart disease, like high blood pressure, goes to the doctor, she is likely to be prescribed medication, which often has the effect of further masking the anger that is partly to blame for the problem, thus making it harder to deal with.

Finally, it's an understatement to say that when we act out of anger, it is likely to be irrational and contrary to our best interests.

An attorney friend was less than a model husband. In fact, he was such a cad that his wife decided to leave him after just a few years. She made her grand exit when he was out of town. She took his Mercedes out of the garage and then rammed it from all four sides with her car. Both cars were totaled as a result, and later when the community property was divided, she was surcharged for the damage to the Mercedes. The greatest irony is that she was angrier after the colossal expression of her rage than she was before.

Western Approaches to Anger

I n our culture, there are three generally practiced approaches to dealing with anger.

First, we can suppress it or, in today's idiom, "stuff it." When a spouse or a boss makes us angry, we are expected to grin and bear it. We may have been so thoroughly conditioned to stifle our anger that we are no longer even aware of its existence.

Second, we can acknowledge the anger, but act it out vicariously. This means that if you are mad at your boss, you may end up venting that anger by lashing out at your spouse, your children, or your pet.

The third conventional route is so-called anger management, which relies on detailed techniques to be used in specific situations, and often includes psychotherapy.

The first option, stuffing it, is generally chosen when dealing with someone who is important to us—our boss, our spouse, or someone else whose good regard is essential to our well-being. The problem with stuffing it is that it keeps the pressure inside, which can do damage to our bodies and psyches. In addition to physiological effects like strokes and heart attacks, suppression requires psychological energy. If we are walking around holding anger inside (like restraining an angry beast), the result is likely to be fatigue and the loss of vital energy for creative pursuits.

When you take your anger out on some unsuspecting third party, that person feels abused for no obvious reason, and gets angry back. Damage to that relationship may create another source of anger in your life.

A once-popular psychotherapeutic remedy for venting anger was to beat on a pillow or yell where no one could hear you. In group therapy, people were supplied with pillows to hit while screaming things like: "Mr. Jones, I hate you!"—whack! "Mr. Jones, you are a son of a bitch!"—whack! and so on. Sometimes people battered one another with foam-rubber batons. All of this went on until you were exhausted. You then sat down with the same satisfied feeling that comes after any workout. Unfortunately, experience showed that while you felt better for a while, like the joke about Chinese food, half an hour later you were still angry. This approach doesn't change your relationship to anger itself; it only serves to temporarily blow off steam. In his book *Anger: Wisdom for Cooling the Flames,* the Vietnamese Buddhist master Thich Nhat Hanh makes an even more incisive criticism: Not only does the venting ritual fail to reduce anger, it serves as a *rehearsal* for physically expressing anger (violently) in the future.

The problem with the third route—psychological intervention—is that it often requires us to regard ourselves as in some way defective or damaged. And consequently we label ourselves as "bad," or "wounded." Although additional insight into oneself is always valuable, this approach is essentially self-accusatory. It says we are not okay. Not only that, but it may take years on the couch and many thousands of dollars to heal us.

The Buddhist approach, as memorably articulated by Pema Chödrön, is "I'm not okay; you're not okay. *It's* okay." We are all flawed human beings, beset by problems and difficulties. We cannot cure our human condition, but Buddhism provides a methodology for undoing our conditioning and, by means of awareness, reducing our suffering.

We return to the question: "Is there an alternative to feeling and expressing anger?"

In the course of this book, I hope to demonstrate that it is possible to reduce the occasions for anger, to deal with it when it arises, and ultimately, to transform anger into compassion.

Difficult as these goals may seem, they can be accomplished. Chapter by chapter, I hope to increase your awareness of the cost of anger, the underlying cause of anger, and the myths and beliefs that perpetuate it.

CHAPTER 2

A First Look at Anger
HOW DOES IT FEEL?

As a first step in learning about anger, let's check out how it actually feels. Take a few minutes to think of some things that made you angry in the past few weeks. These should be unimportant or minor annoyances. A classic irritation is that a spouse leaves the cap off the toothpaste. Or perhaps your kids leave a trail of wet towels on the floor.

Your entries may describe a single, isolated incident or a chronic source of anger: You got angry last week when someone stole a taxicab from you. Or, you are almost invariably angry at other drivers on your daily commute. Write down your anger moments on the following page— both one-time and chronic.

✦ *Exercise*
ONE-TIME THINGS THAT MADE ME ANGRY

✐
_____

_____

_____

_____

_____

_____

_____

✦ THINGS THAT ALWAYS MAKE ME ANGRY

✐
_____

_____

_____

_____

_____

_____

_____

It's important right now not to choose what may be profound sources of anger, such as physical harm inflicted on you or a loved one, your spouse's ongoing infidelity, or being cheated in a Ponzi scheme. Such events may be so mired in feelings of justification and martyrdom—as well as understandable rage—that working with them now is like trying to swim upstream against an overwhelming current. If the lessons of this book become part of your life, however, you may eventually be able to overcome that kind of anger as well.

We have learned from some of the families of victims of the Oklahoma City bombing and the 9/11 tragedy, as well as the victims themselves, that forgiveness of such unspeakable acts is possible. But for now, let's begin with the first, simplest steps.

Success in transforming the anger arising from the most trivial event is empowering. As you discover that you don't need your anger, and that you feel better without it, you can use the same process in dealing with more serious offenses. As Tibetan master Sakyong Mipham says, "The most practical way to ensure forward movement . . . is to train for a short time each day in changing our attitude— just 10 percent. Overdoing it could derail the whole process, like running too far too fast, or lifting more weight than we can bear."

✦ *Exercise* GOING FROM ANGRY TO HAPPY

Close your eyes for a minute or two and recall an incident or event that made you angry, perhaps one you've just listed. Note that you're being asked how you feel *now*, not when the event occurred. Focus on the feeling and don't get caught up in thoughts about whether the offense or your response was justified. Does your pulse race, your blood pressure rise, your temples throb? Do the corners of your mouth turn down, your brow furrow, your muscles tense? You may not remember exactly how you felt in the past; the point is to demonstrate that this event may still have the power to change the way you feel a day, a week, or a year later. Write down how you feel.

Now recall, for a minute or two, some experience or event that made you happy—a birthday party, someone going out of their way to help you, a compliment or a gift. Again, focus on the feeling. Does a smile come to your lips? A feeling of warmth and beneficence overtake you? Really get into the feelings and write them down here.

_____

_____

_____

_____

_____

_____

Compare this to how you felt re-experiencing anger. The lesson of this exercise is pretty obvious: It feels better to be happy than it does to be angry. Anger causes distress. Even if you already agree wholeheartedly with this idea, it's important to vividly experience it now as an emotional baseline for this book. Stopping to experience it will remind you to observe the feelings that arise in your daily life when you are angry, without necessarily having to act upon them.

Now let's shift our awareness to examining how anger arises and why we become angry. What we feel is based to a great degree on what we think. Our assumptions/beliefs affect how we view "reality" and therefore our reaction to it. But what we think or believe can be based on very flimsy evidence. The Milling Exercise (below) is one way to experience this. In a workshop situation, this exercise is enacted in an open, outdoor space with a leader and a group of at least eight people. However, it's possible to imagine the process now and try it out at a later time with a group of friends or at a family picnic.

 ## MILLING EXERCISE

Imagine that you are in a place inhabited by a large number of people. Close your eyes and with your arms at your sides, start milling around slowly. Imagine that you touch another person. When you do, change directions and move quietly on. When you bump into someone, change directions again. Continue like this for a few minutes and note what you experienced and how you felt.

Now, change the rules. Imagine yourself in the same crowded place, again with your eyes closed, so that you cannot avoid touching or bumping into other people. But this time, imagine that everyone is toxic. If you touch someone, you will become injured or ill. Nonetheless, keep moving with your eyes closed. If you brush up against or bump into anyone, break off the contact as quickly as possible. The more you touch others, the worse you will suffer. Be aware of how it feels as you are traveling in this toxic crowd. Write it down.

Now, once again, change the rules. This time, instead of being toxic, everyone is healing and nourishing. Contact is good! The more physical closeness you have, the better you will be. Keep moving with your eyes closed. Be aware of how you feel as you encounter a breast here, a strong forearm there, a quick brush of silken or wrinkled skin. Are you eager to get closer, do you feel sympathy for these beneficial beings? In group workshops, the invariable outcome is that everyone clusters together—sometimes in a mass hug.

....

Compare how you felt in each of the three scenarios in the Milling Exercise, above. In the first, were you wary, curious, neutral?

In the second, when you imagined that everyone was toxic, what changes did you experience in your body? Did you become anxious and pull back, muscles tensed, prepared to flee?

And in the third, did you relax, feel your tension go away, and want to connect? Did touching someone feel welcome?

The usual consensus in the workshops when people share their experiences is that the first phase of the exercise felt awkward. The second created a sense of unease and tension, and the third was characterized by relief and comfort. There are always one or two people in the group who say that they knew the exercise was just a game and weren't affected by the instruction to shift gears in the various phases. But, on further discussion, it usually turns out that even the skeptics were affected by imagining a different scenario.

The first part of the exercise replicates how we feel when we venture outside of our usual, familiar surroundings. We experience the ambiguity that exists in everyday social contact. If you're at a party where you don't know most of the guests, you may feel awkward and at sea. You go to the punch bowl and as you begin pouring a drink, another person approaches and picks up a cup. You offer to fill it for him. He accepts by putting it over the punch bowl. Then your mind begins a nattering internal dialogue: "Gee, he looks interesting. I'd like to talk to him. Maybe he won't want to talk to me. The last time I spoke to a stranger, I was summarily rejected. What can I say that won't seem too forward?"

Often, by the time you decide to comment on how good the punch is, he's already moving off to talk to someone else. Maybe you feel like Linus in the Peanuts cartoon describing his encounter with a little girl he thought was attractive: "I didn't know what to say, so I slugged her."

The second part of the milling exercise demonstrates how quickly and for how little reason the body changes physically, depending on how we think about something. We go from ambivalent or wary to tense, skittish, and fearful, on the basis of only a few words. And in the third part of the exercise, the merest suggestion again changes not only our mood but our entire body.

It is fair to say that everyone would rather live in phase three than in phase two, or even in phase one. So, one of the objectives of this book is to examine the way that suggestion and expectation affect our reality.

The less obvious lesson of the exercise is that the leader occupies the role that our mind plays in everyday life. As in the punch bowl encounter, we are constantly rerunning tapes from yesterday's experiences, our childhoods, or any time in between, interpreting reality according to our own past conditioning. Our minds apply rules of how to engage with a stranger that may have developed when we were three years old and just learning how to play with other toddlers in the sandbox. Most of our thoughts have as little connection to what is happening in the present moment as the suggestion that everyone has suddenly become toxic—or nourishing. This is particularly true when we are engaged in mind reading and think we know what someone else is thinking or what motives underlie a particular action.

Early on in my search to break out of the straitjacket of my life, I was working with a gifted teacher. We were discussing the issue of whether we knew what other people were thinking, when suddenly he rolled over to me in his wheeled office chair and put his nose close up to my face. He then retreated a few feet, and the following dialogue ensued:

"What did I just do?"

I fumbled around for a reply and said, "You were trying to scare me?"

"No."

"You were trying to get my attention?"

"No."

"You were trying to bring me into the here and now?"

"No."

"I give up. What did you just do?"

"I moved closer to you."

This simple demonstration provided me with a sudden insight—or as it's described, "a blinding flash of the obvious." I realized that while I was playing guessing games about my teacher's motives, I was overlooking the obvious. I became aware of the many times that I had ascribed malevolent motives to people even though my thoughts had no basis in reality.

What we observe in the moment is what we know. The

rest is all interpretation based on a filter of past experiences that may or may not have any relevance to it.

The ultimate lesson to be learned from the milling exercise is that we have the power to choose. We needn't be controlled by our previous conditioning or our conventional expectations, but can approach each moment with a fresh, unprejudiced view. You can choose this same transformation in your own life by pausing and asking, "Hey, what's really happening here?"

CHAPTER 3

The Cause of Anger
AN UNMET DEMAND

*wo monks studied under a great master who was
known far and wide for his serenity. One day they got
into an argument. One of them said that the master
sometimes got angry and the other said that the master never
got angry. After much discussion, they decided the only thing
to do was to ask the master. So they went to the master who
was working on a piece of calligraphy and waited quietly until
he looked up. The first monk then said, "Master, I say that
sometimes you get angry, and he says that you never get angry.
Do you get angry?"*

*"Yes and no," said the master, who then looked down and
continued working on his calligraphy.*

The students left and began arguing over the master's answer. They became increasingly agitated over the master's failure to resolve their argument. So they went back to the master and the second monk said, "Master, why do you refuse to answer our question?"

The master said, "I've given each of you the answer you wanted."

The first student said, "We need to know who is right."

"If you know who is right," the master replied, "will that feed or clothe you?"

The student thought for a moment and said, "No master, it will not."

"Why do you choose to suffer?" asked the master.
Whereupon the students felt serenity deeper than the ocean.

◆

The cause of anger is simple: Anger arises when we have an unmet demand. We all make basic demands on the world around us. Some are ongoing, such as the one that others not injure us. Others arise only under special conditions, such as expecting a birthday present or to be left alone when we are working. We make particular demands in particular relationships, such as marriage or work. The demand may be tangible—you expect to be paid for your work—or intangible—you want another person to respect you or love you. However, many of our demands, like the insistence of the monks in the tale above on knowing who is right, may be insignificant and serve only to perpetuate anger in our lives.

Go back to your anger list on page 29 and take a moment to write down the unmet demand underlying each instance you described. For example:

✦ Event	✦ My Unmet Demand
My wife did not remember my birthday.	I expect my wife to remember my birthday.
My husband never puts the cap back on the toothpaste.	I want my husband to respect my desire for a tidy bathroom.
Add some more of your own:	

Whether the event is trivial or significant, the cause of anger is always the same. Underlying the emotional tumult, there is a need that is not being met and that you expect to be met. The demand, in a very broad sense, is the "because" underlying our anger. "I was angry because . . . ."

Note that we use the word "demand" here because it's experienced as an internal demand that we make on the world or a person, and it includes needs, desires, and expectations. Obviously, when we suggest that you voice your "demands," they should be done as requests.

If you can pause to consider what your demand (or need or expectation) is when you feel anger arising, you will have gone a long way toward changing it. Whether or not you follow any of the other suggestions in this book, you will find this simple exercise to be of great value. In fact, certain types of anger may dissolve with no other effort.

More difficulty arises when a seemingly simple event is a manifestation of a deeper issue. In the chart (previous page), both of the examples may more accurately involve the issue of respect. If your spouse does not remember your birthday, you may interpret that as a sign of indifference or lack of love. Similarly, you may interpret your husband's refusal to put the cap back on the toothpaste as indicating lack of respect for your simple requests.

I intentionally said "interpret" to suggest that your

understanding of your husband's behavior may be entirely different from his interpretation or from the truth. He may simply be a slob and may be sloppy in his interactions with the world most of the time. If so, his behavior probably has nothing to do with whether he loves or respects you.

In psychotherapy, you might explore the reasons underlying your demands and expectations. For instance, you might find that you are quick to anger when criticized because your father put you down frequently. The primary goal in psychotherapy is to get to the root cause of the distress; but what we are doing here is not therapy. It is simply learning methods for dealing with and transforming anger. For now, it is enough that you pause and seek out your unmet demand, even on the most superficial level. As you practice becoming aware of your demands, you will find that you are able to identify the cause of your anger with greater accuracy and honesty. Success in doing this will reduce the intensity and frequency of anger and some of the distress that accompanies it. Then more accurate insights into what motivates us occur without special effort.

It's not as important that you identify the *correct* demand as it is that you pause to ask yourself what it is. The pause, in and of itself, reduces your anger. As you learn to identify your real demands, you may choose to abandon them or learn how to get them met more effectively.

The Four Types of Demands

Our demands fall into four general types. Like all classifications, this one does not pretend to be the last word but provides a starting place for looking at the subject more deeply.

- **The Important and Reasonable Demand**

  You want your partner to love you.

  This type is entirely justifiable and significant.

- **The Reasonable but Unimportant Demand**

  You want to be seated by the window at a restaurant; you want to eat Chinese, she wants to eat Italian.

  Although reasonable, this demand may really not be so important, now that you examine it.

- **The Irrational Demand**

  You don't want to put up with traffic annoyances. You want respect from a stranger.

  When you look at it, this demand is silly or unreasonable.

- **The Impossible Demand**

  "I want people to accept my wisdom" or *"I want everyone to love me." "Make me happy"* or *"I want you to fix everything that's wrong with my life."*

  Demands in this category are usually ongoing rather than occasioned by a single incident, and are expressed in terms of generalities. This type of expectation, because it can't be met, provides the justification for ongoing anger and is the basis for a chronic renunciation of happiness.

Go back again to your anger chart on page 41. Decide how you would classify the demands underlying each of the incidents you listed. Do some of them fall into the categories of Irrational, Impossible, or Unimportant? When similar provocations arise, pause and consider whether you might be able to drop any anger attached to them.

Unspoken Demands

One way that we invite anger into our lives is by not letting our demands be known. We expect, in fact, that people around us magically know what we want from them. When they do not divine our needs, we get angry. Consider the following:

Imagine that you just bought a pair of expensive pants and the first time you wore them, they ripped. When you go back to the store to return the pants, what do you say to the person at the counter?

"Look at these pants. They ripped."

"Uh-huh."

"They're shoddy goods."

"Uh-huh."

"You should be ashamed of yourselves selling goods like this."

"Uh-huh."

"I want my money back."

"At last."

Don't be one of those angry people who go around expecting loved ones to read their minds and then get furious when their unspoken demand is not divined and met. That kind of person often labors under another expectation: If you really cared [loved me], you would *know* what I want.

In my anger workshop, I ask people to turn to the person next to them, preferably a stranger, not someone they may have attended with, and make a simple demand involving some physical contact, like a neck rub. The reason for the physical contact is to avoid making a routine demand like asking to borrow a pen. The person being asked may or may not choose to comply. Then the roles are reversed. Is it easier to make a demand or to comply with one? The almost universal experience in the workshop is that meeting a specific demand is easier than making one.

In everyday life, there is usually an ongoing exchange involved in meeting one another's needs. Experiment with this on your own by asking another person to meet a specific request. For instance, you are behind a person with a large

basket of items at the checkout counter. You have only one
or two items and are in a hurry. Ask if you can go ahead.
You are having a hard time loading something into your car.
Ask a stranger for help.

Unstated Demands

A re there unstated demands in your life that might be
met if you made the request? Are they reasonable?
Important? Do you get angry when someone doesn't meet
one of your implicit demands? Do you perpetuate your anger
by refusing to ask for what you want? Take a moment to think
of a few of your unstated demands and enter them below.

_____

_____

_____

_____

_____

_____

Practice in making requests and examining the nature
of our unspoken demands may help illuminate many of our
occasions for anger.

The unwillingness to articulate what we really want or need causes major difficulties in intimate relationships. Couples therapy often addresses this issue by teaching people how to articulate their underlying demands.

◆

During a Friday marriage counseling session, a woman told her husband that she would like him to give her flowers, not because it was her birthday or their anniversary, but simply as an expression of his affection. The next week, the husband called the florist and had a splendid bouquet sent to her with a note saying, "I love you." In their next counseling session, he had assumed he'd finally done something right. Instead, his wife was offended because although he had sent the flowers, he hadn't signed the card.

The wife obviously had a number of unspoken demands:

Her husband should know, without being asked, to give her presents from time to time for no particular reason.

If she has to ask for a gift, it doesn't count.

If her husband gives her a gift, he should not simply order it over the phone but should take the trouble to personalize it.

The wife's desire for a kind of sensitivity and intimacy that's expressed by spontaneous gift-giving may not have been part of the husband's experience.

She might have chosen to appreciate the gift rather than look at what was lacking. Instead of becoming angry, she might have said, "Thank you for the beautiful bouquet." By rewarding his efforts, she might have created warmth between the two of them that led to greater intimacy.

Many relationships are in jeopardy because one or more of the participants has unmet demands that he or she is either unaware of or unwilling to voice. These may include relationships between spouses, lovers, neighbors, business partners, or members of an organization. The more important the relationship—a marriage versus membership in a book club, for instance—the more the parties have to lose. Where there is a lot to lose, people may be less likely to make their demands explicit because the risk of doing so is greater.

One spouse may fear that if the other knows how needy she or he is, it may damage the relationship. Another common fear is: "If people really know who I am, or what I want, they will shun me or worse." A third is the fear that the other person will refuse to satisfy the demand and the feeling of rejection that will ensue.

Articulating your desires may be an essential first step to fulfilling them, but it doesn't guarantee that they will be met. Sometimes people may keep their demands to themselves because they understand that voicing them is too risky. For instance, a husband may have a desire that his wife shouldn't object if he has a mistress. In this case, the relationship is not likely to be improved by voicing the demand. The wife, on her part, may expect that the husband honor his marriage vows and remain faithful to her. The restraint on both sides of not stating their underlying desires may be all that's keeping the relationship intact.

It may, however, be constructive to end a relationship in which significant demands can't be met. Often, we continue in relationships that are not meeting our needs out of a sense of scarcity. That is, we are unwilling to take the risk of leaving the relationship we have, believing that we won't be able to find one that better suits our needs. Freezing our lives in place is another way we perpetuate anger.

There is no rule that says we have to let other people know our demands. We may choose not to disclose them. However, we should be aware of the possible consequences of keeping our needs to ourself.

✦ *Exercise* STATE YOUR NEEDS

Are there any needs that you expect to be met that you have not stated to the important people in your life? List them here. It may help to think of the important people in your life one at a time and whether you are harboring any anger or dissatisfaction toward them and if so, why.

_____

_____

_____

_____

_____

_____

_____

_____

_____

Examine each of your demands and ask yourself whether it might be met if you voiced it. Have you failed to express it because of a fear about doing so, or because you assume the other person should know without being told? Do you unconsciously expect your partner, or whoever is involved, to be able to read your mind?

Experiment with making requests—perhaps not all at once, but one at a time. If you are unwilling, for some reason, to reveal what you want, ask yourself whether your reason is a valid one. If it is, you will at least understand your role and responsibility in the anger you feel when it is not met. In other words, it's important to recognize that you have a choice and are not helpless to act in the situation.

Failing to articulate our needs and desires can serve to keep us isolated and lonely. Many single people complain that they cannot find a satisfactory partner or relationship. Perhaps they fail to do so because they are unwilling to express their desires with the result that potential significant others are left in the dark. I call this The Flight Path Theory of Relationships:

You can land at my airport, but don't come in too fast or too slow, too far to the right or to the left, too high or too low. However, I am not going to tell you what any of the parameters are. And if you do succeed in landing once, don't expect the parameters to be the same the next time. Realizing that you have a complex and secret flight path to your heart may produce sadness rather than anger. But it also offers the possibility of change.

Another expectation that sets us up for failure and disappointment is that we want our relationships to be perfect. Our definition of perfection may come from our obsolete rules and baggage. In an otherwise good marriage, a husband may be angry because his wife doesn't like to cook. She is a great mother and wage earner, and he enjoys her company. But he carries around this expectation and is resentful every time they eat frozen dinners or go out to eat.

A wife may demand a high standard of living which requires that her husband work long hours. She may then be mad because he doesn't spend more time at home. Viewing the relationship as a whole instead of focusing on the part that seems deficient may immediately improve the situation. Again, it's necessary to examine and understand your role and responsibility in the problem.

The issues underlying your demands are individual and complex. They cannot be solved by packaged formulas. But reducing the amount of anger resulting from not recognizing and voicing your desires will empower you to address them when you decide to do so.

CHAPTER 4

The Cost of Anger
WHO PAYS?

*Using anger to solve a problem is like grabbing
a red-hot coal to throw at the other person.*

—Tibetan Proverb

*O*nce a man was consumed with anger at another
man. Day and night he was agitated by his anger,
which left him constantly unhappy. One day a
friend came to see him, and when he saw the state he was in,
the friend asked, "Why are you so bothered all the time? What
has made you grow so thin?"

The man answered, "There is a man in this village who
spoke ill of me and I have not been able to get back at him.
I want to kill him for injuring me, and it is driving me crazy
trying to think of a way to do it."

His friend said, "A demon's curse can kill this man. I can
teach it to you, but it has a major disadvantage: when you kill
him, you will also be killed."

When the first man heard this he was not disturbed.
"I beg you, teach me the curse. Even if it causes my death,
at least it will kill him, too."

—A Flock of Fools

✦

Nothing is more costly than anger and, as the tale of the
demonic curse illustrates, some people are willing to pay the
ultimate price in order to express their hatred toward others.
If we tallied up all the deaths caused by road rage, barroom
brawls, heart attacks, and war, which Buddhist scholar
Robert Thurman calls "organized anger," we might find that
this deadly sin kills more people than anything else.

Short of death, nothing can maim, harm, and alienate
us from others like anger. A moment of anger can destroy a
lifelong friendship or a reputation, or blunt the career we've
spent many years building. Chronic anger can create lifelong
problems in our children. It can destroy our effectiveness
and make our daily lives miserable. Anger builds when
repressed and continues to roil the mind until it finally
succumbs. We've all had nights when we tossed and turned,
seething, because we carried into bed with us the anger from
something that happened earlier in the day. In the case of

a particularly horrific incident, we may carry that anger for days, months, or even a lifetime, with continuing damage to our psyches and bodies. If we express that anger, we may inflict pain, not only on the intended object of our rage, but also on those who might be indirectly affected in the future. When we're angry we become oblivious to how other people will feel about and respond to that anger, but the so-called collateral damage can be considerable.

The Price We Pay Directly

To begin with, it doesn't feel good to be angry. So the first cost of anger is its effect on our own minds and bodies. If we felt the effects for only a short time, the damage wouldn't be so bad. But anger has a way of lingering and festering. My wife was working at her catering kitchen one day when a young man came in. He said that he had run out of gas and asked if she would lend him twenty dollars. He showed her a driver's license which revealed him to be a member of a prominent local family, and wrote her an IOU for the money. When a few days passed with no sign of the young man, she called the number on the IOU. The person who answered was a member of the prominent family but said that there was no such young man. My wife, who is not much given to anger, was furious that he had taken advantage of her trust and generosity. Every time someone handed her a twenty dollar bill that week the anger returned, distracting her from whatever she was doing. As author Hugh Prather said, "Holding onto anger is giving someone else free rent in our head."

The Price to Our Relationships

Merely carrying anger around with us can be costly, but if we express it toward others, the price escalates. If you are working at home and the kids are noisy, yelling at them in a violent outburst may shut them up. But your children learn to fear you. If your significant other proposes buying something you don't think you can afford, anger may put an end to the argument sooner than reason will, but there's a rift in the relationship. If you are able to bully a business associate into agreeing to your terms by means of anger, you may in fact get a better deal than you would have otherwise. But next time, he may be a tougher adversary or refuse to deal with you altogether.

The question remains: Even if your short-term goal is met, is the cost to the relationship too great, whether it be a family, romantic, or business one, to warrant the use of anger? Put most simply: People don't like angry people, and they resent being the target of anger.

Because anger arises from an unmet demand, its ostensible purpose is to fulfill that demand. However, from a rational perspective, it's often quite useless in achieving this. The use of anger to get our way earlier in our lives may have rewarded this tactic. The child who learned to manipulate her parents by throwing a tantrum may carry this technique into adulthood. But anger is probably not going to be an effective tool for getting what you want in the present.

Compare the following scenarios:

1. A man says to the waiter at a busy restaurant, "Look, we have tickets to the theater, and we have to be out of here in forty-five minutes. If we aren't, then your boss is going to hear about it."

Or:

2. The man says to the waiter: "We have a problem. We have tickets to the theater, and we need to be finished in forty-five minutes. Can you help?"

Who gets the faster service? As someone at one of my workshops commented, "They might both make it to the theater on time, but the first couple might have something besides soup in their soup."

An employee makes a mistake. Compare the following reactions from a boss:

1. "Boy was that dumb. I can't imagine anyone would do something as stupid as that. See that it doesn't happen again."

Or:

2. "Look, apparently you made a mistake. We all make mistakes. What can we do so it doesn't happen again?"

In the response of the first boss, not only does the employee have to acknowledge that she made a mistake, but she also has to absorb the insult of being told that she's stupid. Again, which employee is less likely to repeat the same error?

Some years ago, when I had a brief fling at being a bridge player, I didn't fare too well until I read a book called *Why You Lose at Bridge*. I still remember the principle that when your partner makes a bonehead play like trumping your ace and you chew him out for it, you have assured yourself of future bonehead plays. That one insight greatly improved my game.

One positive example: A client whom I have represented for many years is a good and honest businessman. However, he does have a temper. One day he came storming into my office holding a rental tax assessment from the city. He owned an incorporated business and a building which, for various reasons, he leased to his business without paying rental tax. The city was claiming that tax was now due for the previous fifteen years. The bill came to about $33,000 with an ominous reference to interest and penalties that could have doubled that amount. I researched the law and found that, unfortunately for him, the city was completely correct.

We discussed what to do, and I suggested that he go down to City Hall alone and beg for mercy. Since there were no legal issues to be raised, the presence of an attorney might be interpreted as a veiled threat and might make the city less sympathetic. As it happened, I was giving my workshop that weekend and I suggested that he attend, which he did. The following Monday, he met with the city auditor. After an hour, she said: "Well, I think we can get rid of this for under $10,000." He thanked her profusely.

Then she said, "You know, Mr. Smith, I wanted to do something nice for you. Everyone who comes down to see me is angry and you weren't." My client later told me that his only problem at that point was not cracking up laughing—at himself, of course.

Incredibly, people operate under the illusion that they can force someone to do something simply by using anger. They relentlessly throw their finest sarcasm and indignation at someone like a public employee, who is neither responsible for the situation nor at all interested in receiving abuse. This attitude can only increase the employee's resolve to carry out the letter of the law with total indifference to the attacker's suffering.

Unfortunately, the employee's pleasure in foiling you is part of the anger equation. The term *schadenfreude* describes the pleasure some people feel at the pain of those whom they perceive as having wronged them. This is one of the mechanisms that increases the likelihood that your release of anger will come back to harm you. As it is said, "As you sow, so shall you reap."

Anger Makes Us Act Stupidly

Okay, sometimes we may get our way by means of anger, but by becoming angry, we put ourselves at an immediate disadvantage by abandoning our intelligence. The fact that anger makes us act stupidly is not a learned response but is in fact the way the brain works. Groundbreaking research by New York University neuroscientist Joseph E. LeDoux confirms that anger arises in a small, primitive part of the brain called the amygdala (where the fight-or-flight response originates). The amygdala's response is automatic and instantaneous—it's so quick that the prefrontal lobe, where logic and reason reside, can't move fast enough to override these intense emotions. In terms of primitive survival, this was a good thing. If you were being charged by a mastodon, the faster you could react the better. But when it comes to anger, the amygdala's reaction is often too much, too soon, leaving our rational brain behind in the dust. In other words, when we are in the throes of anger, we don't have access to our rational faculties, which helps explain why we often act stupidly when we act out of anger. Later, after an outburst, we often say, "What was I thinking?" Well, the point is, you weren't.

In anger, the prefrontal lobe is further compromised by what University of California, Los Angeles, neuroscientist Matthew D. Lieberman has identified as an inverse relationship between the two areas of the brain. All that blood and oxygen rushing to fuel your amygdala's angry tirade leaves your prefrontal lobe particularly sluggish. In other words, if your amydgala and prefrontal lobe were in a shoot-out, the amygdala's gun would have gone off while the prefrontal lobe was still loading.

When reason takes a backseat to our compulsion to vent our feelings, that severely reduces our chances of a beneficial outcome. If we limit our options to those arising out of anger, we compromise our ability to achieve the best resolution to any situation.

A common source of anger in today's world is the literal-minded computer that I, like many others, have come to depend on. Computers, for no good reason, may suddenly freeze up and not respond to commands. You then have to shut them down. When they restart, a punitive message appears on the screen to the effect: "You have not shut your computer down properly, and therefore we will proceed to scan for the damage caused." Every time this happened to me, I would fume during the wait, barely controlling my impulse to throw the computer out the window.

Then one day I was working with a friend when the computer froze up. He shut it down and started it up again. When the message appeared, he pushed the X key and the normal boot-up commenced. I realized that all along I had allowed a metal box to enrage me rather than trying to find a rational solution.

The result of expressing our anger at an object may be comical in its futility. When an object fails us, we may hit it or kick it, perhaps injuring ourselves. But more serious problems arise when the source of our anger is a person rather than an object.

An object can't respond to an attack, but a person may fire back if we've had the audacity to suggest that she has failed us or might have done better. For good measure, she may retaliate by escalating the level of hostility. That type of exchange might look something like this:

A: "Well you really screwed up on that one."

B: "I screwed up? If you had given me the information in time, this wouldn't have happened."

A: "Me give you the information? You jerk, that was your responsibility."

B: "It's never your fault. You always shift the blame and retreat into your smug little world."

A: "You're a hopeless jerk. I never want to talk to you again."

Notice that what started with the criticism of a specific act ends up with each person totally writing off the other, at least as far as having a place in his or her future endeavors. Rather than ending the exchange of anger, the conversation leaves each combatant unsatisfied. Although neither person is likely to acknowledge it, what really happened is that they both lost. They have not only terminated a relationship, at least temporarily, but also built an additional barrier to restoring it.

One day when I was filling my car with gas, a woman with a small child came out of the Circle K. He was crying, and she was yelling, "I don't care what you do, I'm getting in the car and going home." I assumed that he was screaming because he wanted an ice-cream cone or candy and she wouldn't buy it for him. The child, still crying, got into the backseat obediently and buckled his safety belt. The woman started the car and turned back to him, continuing to scold. The car went forward and hit a post.

"Now look what you made me do!" she yelled.

Out of anger, this woman made several self-destructive errors. She drove forward while looking backward, which speaks for itself. She blamed someone else for her mistake, which is a recipe for future trouble. If we do not recognize our role in our misfortune, we are unable to change the conduct that led to it, which almost guarantees that it will happen again. And, she didn't consider the effect her anger could have on her child, ranging from the destruction of his happiness and self-esteem to setting a bad example for how to deal with life's frustrations.

A saying comes to mind: Anger is as good at solving problems as a fan is at stacking papers.

The Physics of Anger

When I studied physics in college, the concept of a chain reaction was demonstrated using mousetraps in a closed box with one wall made of glass. On the floor of the box were traps set and ready to snap. Instead of the usual piece of cheese, there were two marbles sitting on each trap. When the first trap was sprung, the two marbles hit two other traps that then launch four marbles, which triggered eight more, and so on. In a very short time, the box was filled with flying marbles. A principle of physics mandates the chain reaction for marbles. It is an equally reliable principle that the expression of anger triggers a chain reaction.

The all-too-usual scenario is that the expression of anger toward another arouses similar feelings in return. Retaining anger is uncomfortable or painful and the person on the receiving end may retaliate toward her attacker. But if that's not possible, she may discharge her anger toward other people, even if they had nothing to do with the incident.

A common variation occurs when you cannot direct the anger back at the source because that person is your boss, or your spouse, or as in traffic incidents, not in your physical presence. The resulting stored anger may then be vented on whomever we feel free to abuse.

This type of venting provides no satisfaction as you still haven't confronted the person who made you angry in the first place. Instead there's a chain reaction, beginning perhaps when A, the boss, expresses anger at B. B, who cannot retaliate at his boss, is now holding the anger energy and looking for a place to release it. B may vent his anger at his subordinates, C and D. They cannot return the anger, and so they go home and take it out on their significant others, the kids, or the dog. Only the dog, having a Buddhist nature, doesn't carry the process onward. So one angry person becomes two, and the two become four, and so on.

In my wife's family they use the expression "third-beared" to describe the situation when you are unwittingly caught up in someone else's drama. Two bears are at a garbage dump; the first bear is atop the heap helping himself to delights when the second bear begins to muscle in on the action. The number one bear turns and attacks the number two bear who hastily retreats. On the way out, the number two bear passes a third bear who is minding his own business and whacks him upside the head. So when anger comes someone's way for no good reason, my in-laws say: "You just got third-beared."

When waves of anger from different sources intersect, they are likely to be further amplified. The result is an angry society. It is not difficult to imagine the anger energy we set in motion making a full circle and coming back at us.

The Buddha said:

Speak not harshly to anyone,
For those thus spoken to, might retort.
*   Indeed, angry speech hurts,*
And retribution may overtake you.

How Anger Spills Over to Others

What about the people who are not part of the angry exchange? A person who has just had a fit of anger and then drives a car is a hazard to the world around him. But his anger alienates him not only from other anonymous drivers, but from those he must deal with on a more intimate basis.

Experienced trial lawyers tell their witnesses that they should never become angry on the stand. To do so risks alienating the jury. If someone is known to have a bad temper or to be an angry person, other people will try to avoid dealing with him or her. Chronic anger keeps people at a distance and may even isolate us from others. They may be our spouses, children, or long-time friends, none of whom understands why you are angry at them. We all know that people would rather not deal with an angry person. Nevertheless, some continue to behave as if this truism applies to everyone but them.

The boss who becomes angry at every mistake an employee makes is likely to find that productivity falls and turnover rises. After all, who wants to take direction from a chronically angry person? The husband who is always criticizing his wife may find that the relationship continues but on an alienated basis. As someone commented in a workshop, "You may be getting laid, but you're not getting loved."

The angry energy we broadcast does not go away even though we may no longer be angry ourselves. In effect, each time anger is acted out it achieves a life of its own. In a way, it pollutes the environment. We dump chemicals in a river thinking they will dissipate. When they come back to haunt us, we claim we were unaware of their effect. Anger, like pollution, accumulates and has toxic consequences.

In one episode of *Star Trek*, an alien entity came aboard the ship. It was terribly powerful and incited violence between the two crews. When it was attacked, it became even more destructive. Kirk figured out that it was drawing energy from the crew's negative emotions. When everyone just laughed at it, it got weaker and weaker and finally dissipated. That's a good metaphor for dealing with anger. It's like the old peace slogan: Suppose they gave a war and nobody came?

When we are angry, we believe that we can set things right only by triumphing over our opponent. When anger is directed at us, we are conditioned to become angry ourselves. We assume that because someone insulted us, we *should* be angry. But there is no law that says this. Greater happiness and well-being are achieved by another route.

CHAPTER 5

Anger and Awareness
WHO *ME* ANGRY?

Two monks, Tanzan and Ekido, were traveling down a muddy road. A heavy rain was falling. Coming around a bend, they met a lovely girl in a silk kimono and obi who was unable to cross the road. "Come on, girl," said Tanzan at once. Lifting her in his arms, he carried her over the mud.

For two hours Tanzan and Ekido continued walking in silence, as is the monks' practice when outside their temple. When the temple was in sight, Ekido could no longer restrain himself: "We monks don't go near females," he told Tanzan. "I can't believe you actually touched a woman—no, actually embraced her."

"I put her down two hours ago," said Tanzan. "Are you still carrying her?"

Despite his training in Zen, the monk Ekido in "The Tale of Two Monks" was unaware that he was carrying anger. We can be profoundly and perhaps continually angry without realizing or acknowledging it even when it's totally obvious to others as it was to Ekido's fellow monk Tanzan. It always gets a good laugh when someone says to a red-faced friend who is shouting, "Well, you don't have to get angry," and he responds, "I'm not angry! What makes you think I'm angry?"

Many forces conspire to make us suppress anger and hide it from ourselves. The early days in psychotherapy are often punctuated by the therapist saying, "Didn't that make you angry?" with the client protesting, "Oh, no, I wasn't angry," until eventually the mask falls.

Some of us grew up in families where it wasn't permissible to express angry feelings. Others may be unwilling to admit their anger because they intuit that anger is wrong and therefore they're ashamed to cop to it. They may also be afraid of what they might do, or that others might react in kind, if they were to openly express anger. In the expression popularized today by Dr. Phil, they do not want to "own" their anger or the demands that may underlie it. They want to preserve the illusion that they are totally altruistic people, acting on the best possible motives, who would never give in to such a base emotion.

Another factor that inhibits acknowledging anger is the fear that it may run away with you. But the contrary is true. It's the anger we don't admit to that frequently leads to the statement, "I don't know what came over me." Not only does denial destroy the possibility of dealing with anger, but it is likely to make useful communication all but impossible. Yet, anger will nevertheless emerge indirectly or in disguise. Consider the following scenarios:

- On a date with a doctor, a woman finds herself telling him how wonderfully other men have treated her in the past. Later, when she mentions that she wants to have acupuncture to treat her back pain, he says, "Acupuncture has never helped anyone. Why don't you just go to church? It would be just as effective and less expensive."

- A man who has just broken up with his girlfriend suddenly becomes accident-prone. He drops an iron skillet on his foot, hits his finger when he's hammering a nail, and drives over a cement barrier when he's leaving a parking place.

- A woman who has moved to another city makes a Saturday night date, a month in advance, with a friend in her old hometown. When she arrives on her visit, she calls her friend to ask if they can meet on Friday instead. The friend agrees. On Friday morning the visiting friend calls and asks to move the date a half hour earlier, to 6 P.M.

The hometown friend goes to the restaurant at the new time, but then gets a call from the visitor saying she's running late. When the visitor arrives at 6:45, the friend says, "We were supposed to meet at 6." The visitor blows up and says, "If you're going to be angry, let's just forget it!" and gets up to leave.

• A man proves his taste and discernment by criticizing every experience. The book wasn't that good; the movie could have been better; the restaurant is overpriced; his friend's new girlfriend isn't that pretty.

Do you recognize yourself in any of these scenarios? They are all expressions of anger—whether conscious or unconscious. The well-known phenomenon called "passive aggression," in which negative feelings are expressed in passive ways like sullenness or intentional inefficiency, is one of these. The person behaving this way, like the woman in the example above who was late and then guilt-tripped her friend, may be unaware of her hostile feelings and of the damage such behavior may cause. Likewise someone who smokes cigars around other people or rides a motorcycle with an aggressively loud muffler may be unconscious of the offense. Sometimes the underlying anger may break through as in the famous joke about so-called Freudian slips: "I meant to say, 'Please pass the salt,' but instead I said, 'You bitch, you've ruined my life.'"

Another way unacknowledged anger sometimes emerges is in actions that are harmful to oneself or randomly destructive, such as dropping something, spilling the soup, or becoming accident-prone. Chronic depression can also be a manifestation of anger that is persistently turned inward or expressed against the self.

Some people are chronically angry but express it through the socially acceptable mode of criticism—their judgment and taste are better than that of others—or via cynicism. In a marriage or friendship, chronic criticism will almost certainly cast a dark cloud over the relationship. Directed against one's children, it may seriously erode their self-esteem and lead to apathy and underachievement or hatred and outright aggression. For some people, this critical mode of being is so pervasive that it constitutes their essential personality.

Although it's far easier to recognize these patterns in others, try to recognize anger in yourself and the ways in which you may indirectly express it. Becoming aware of anger is essential to any change, and sometimes the mere act of observing it can enable you to drop at least some instances of it on the spot. Some dieters who keep food diaries often find that simply writing down what they are eating throughout the day causes the pounds to fall off. The Smoke Enders exercise of wrapping a piece of paper around your cigarette pack and writing down the time and what you were feeling when you reached for a smoke can go a long way toward reducing the habit. So the first step is to own your anger. As long as you don't act on it, no one but you will keep score no matter how many times a day you get angry.

✦ *Exercise* OWN YOUR ANGER

So go ahead. Think back over the last twenty-four hours. Were there times when you were angry or whatever name you call it such as irritated, offended, or impatient? Don't analyze or judge whether the feeling was appropriate or justified. Just note the essence of what happened: "Woman talking on cell phone driving erratically," or "Kate grabbing more than her share of the crab appetizer." Write down as many things as you can think of.

Knowing When You're Angry

In Chapter 3, we learned that the cause of anger is an unmet demand. Stopping to ask, "What is my demand here?" can be a key to recognizing our anger. Sometimes we suppress the anger and don't acknowledge it. Yet we feel that something isn't quite right. We might experience a sense that we are not responding correctly. For example, we might brush off our landlord's failure to pay a bill that results in the electricity being turned off with a casual remark like, "Well, mistakes happen." That would be great if we really meant it. But instead, we might find our blood pressure rising every time we think of the incident. This may be a symptom of anger that we did not acknowledge and deal with.

The unconscious subtext may be, "Why do I always have to be the good guy?" "Why am I always the victim?" In this kind of situation, rerunning the incident and considering if you have an unmet demand may bring the cause and fact of your anger into consciousness. Then you can begin processing the anger.

Sometimes, as well as feeling uneasy, we experience physical manifestations of anger—clenched fists, increased blood pressure, a rapid pulse, a surge of adrenaline, gritted teeth, or tensed muscles. We need to tune into these physical sensations and give them their due. Our most basic and universal way of expressing anger, however, is via speech. Verbal abuse and aggression can be as dangerously provocative as a slap or a blow. This can include the outright curses and obscenities that punctuate angry exchanges, as well as racial slurs and other varieties of name-calling. Stereotyping—"All lawyers are greedy," "All Muslims are terrorists"—betrays anger at a group or one of its members.

Sarcasm always indicates anger—"I *knew* you'd do that." "Is *that* what you call doing a good job?" Derision and ridicule is often expressed by intonation. "My, what a pretty dress that is," may be a compliment or an insult depending on where the emphasis is placed.

Humor can be used as a way of indirectly expressing hostility, if not anger, as the endless jokes about blondes, Poles or other ethnic groups, or the opposite sex attest.

"If a man is talking in the forest and there's no woman to hear him, is he still wrong?"

Or this one from the other side of the gender divide:

"Why did the Israelites wander in the desert for forty years?"

"Because even then, men wouldn't ask for directions."

Even silence, or the withdrawal of all communication, can be an expression of seething, underlying anger as in the well-known "silent treatment."

✦ *Exercise* HOW DO *YOU* EXPRESS ANGER?

Now that we've looked at some of the more subtle ways anger disguises itself, can you recall any ways you may habitually express it, despite not being fully aware of what you were doing? Are there phrases you use? Gestures?

Perhaps you now have a few more items to add to your anger list.

✎
_____

_____

_____

_____

_____

_____

Varieties of Anger

Whereas in the western world, anger may be considered a sin (even though it may be employed by a wrathful God), in Eastern philosophy it is considered an addiction, one of three root poisons (along with greed and delusion) that cause suffering. In his teachings, the Buddha described anger as having a "golden crest and a poisoned root." While its addictive quality makes it appear attractive, it's a double-edged sword, wounding not only the person who is its object but also, from within, the one who wields it.

Ancient Buddhist teachers recognized an entire range of attitudes—irritation, annoyance, disapproval, impatience, dividing the world into friend and foe, a strong attachment to one's own views and opinions, one's likes and dislikes—as part and parcel of the anger addiction because they lead to, and at any moment can flare into, rage. In Tibetan there's a word, *shenpa*, that refers to the charge, the addictive quality, behind our likes and dislikes. Someone who doesn't agree with you is "a thorn in your side." "You can be committed to peace, or to environmental causes," says American Buddhist nun Pema Chödrön, "but you may be peace marchers clubbing one another with your likes and dislikes. It doesn't matter how right we are, we're still strengthening a pattern of aggression." We stop seeing the other person as a person, and instead see them as a problem or foe. "It's just one opinion against another opinion, but this is the sustenance of war, of cruelty."

Becoming Aware

Anger is an obstruction that keeps us from taking advantage of the whole cornucopia of life before us. Greater awareness—simply noting our habitual patterns without judgment—can reduce the amount of anger in our lives, which, in turn, frees us to notice more dispassionately what is happening to us and sets the stage for change.

As we've discussed earlier, the very essence of Buddhism is awareness—being alive and alert in the present. Most often when we are "thinking," we are thinking about what has happened in the past, or what may happen in the future, rather than directly experiencing what is happening now. We are manipulating abstract concepts, planning our "to do" list, or calculating how to achieve our next goal.

We've probably all had the experience of missing our turn when driving, only to realize it several miles down the road. We search vainly for our sunglasses, only to find them perched on top of our heads. We are not fully present in mind *or* body.

One evening, some friends came over for dinner and were regaling us with tales about their recent visit to New York and how outrageously expensive it was. The husband told of a meal for six at a classy restaurant that had cost $1,400. My daughter gasped and said, "My God, what did you have?" The husband paused a moment and said, "I don't remember." Apparently, he was so caught up in calculating the price tag that he didn't even taste the food.

In a classic experiment, some adults were asked to watch a video of several people tossing a ball around and were told to count how many passes particular people made. In the midst of the video, a person in a gorilla suit walked slowly through the group of ballplayers. A surprising number of the subjects were so intent on their assignment that they didn't notice the unexpected appearance of the gorilla at all.

Commenting on the intelligence of babies, Alison Gopnik, a professor of psychology at the University of California, Berkeley, explained the adults' blindness to the gorilla by the fact that, as we grow and develop, we learn to become goal-oriented and therefore to focus only on observing what's most pragmatically useful to us. Babies, on the other hand, are captivated by those events that are most unexpected; they are drawn to anything new or unusual from which they can learn. "Babies explore, adults exploit," Gopnik summarizes.

In Buddhist terms, adults lose what Sunryu Suzuki, one of the founders of American Zen, calls "original mind." In *Zen Mind, Beginner's Mind*, he writes: "Our 'original mind' includes everything within itself. It is always rich and sufficient within itself. You should not lose your self-sufficient state of mind. This does not mean to suggest a closed mind, but rather an empty mind and a ready mind. If your mind is empty, it is always ready for anything; it is open to everything. . . . In the beginner's mind there are many possibilities; in the expert's mind there are few."

✦ WATCH IT

Are you wearing a watch? If so, start by covering it with your hand. Now answer the following questions:

What does your watch look like? Is there any text printed or inscribed on it? Are the numerals Roman, Arabic, or just slash marks? Is there a separate second-hand dial or a sweep second hand?

Look at your watch. How accurately did you remember it?

Now cover your watch again.

What time is it?

Despite the fact that most people have looked at their watches thousands of times, very few pass this test. They don't do well on describing their timepieces, and almost no one has noticed the time. This is a small common example of our general lack of awareness.

When we have lost "original mind," and our brains are filled with categories, classifications, prejudices, and conditioned responses, we are unlikely to respond spontaneously to events or to our interactions with others. We become angry automatically without actually perceiving what is happening to us and therefore we become incapable of learning something new or responding freshly to the actual moment.

In an essay called "For the Time Being," Zoketsu Norman Fischer, a poet and former co-abbot of the San Francisco Zen Center, writes, "Most of us don't know what it actually feels like to be alive. We know about our problems, our desires, our goals and accomplishments, but we don't know much about our lives. It generally takes a huge event, the equivalent of a birth or a death, to wake up our sense of living this moment we are given—this moment that is just for the time being, because it passes even as it arrives." He concludes: "To really live is to accept that you live 'for the time being,' and to fully enter that moment of time. Living is that, not building up an identity or a set of accomplishments or relationships, though of course we do that too. But primarily, fundamentally, to live is to embrace each moment as if it were the first, last, and all moments of time."

The process of becoming less angry and more aware is a two-way street. Reducing anger creates a self-reinforcing cycle: As we become less angry, we become more aware of what is actually happening as opposed to judging what is happening. As we become more aware, we become less angry.

One source of anger is that the same bad things keep happening to us. We may even imagine the world is conspiring against us. We can't maintain a relationship, keep a job, or retain our clients. When we experience such losses for the first time, we may grin and bear it. But when we suffer defeat over and over again, we become angry at life. Although bad things *do* happen to good people and sometimes success is achieved only when we persevere through many defeats, the reason we fail repeatedly may be that we keep acting out of the same rules or old habits. As Albert Einstein said, "Insanity is doing the same thing over and over again and expecting different results."

On the other hand, if we increase our awareness of our habitual patterns, we open up the possibility of change. Earlier in my life, I went to one encounter weekend after another. I came out of many of them on a temporary high. However, I didn't change in any essential way and soon reverted to type. I remained the same hostile control freak, with anger as my prime directive. What I realized was that, in a group of strangers, I let go of many of my habitual behaviors. But when I returned to the "real" world and the usual stresses of my environment, my habits reasserted themselves, and with them, the same old problems.

In Buddhism, one of the main practices for undoing our conditioning by increasing our awareness, or what is called "right mindfulness," is the practice of long periods of seated meditation or *zazen*.

The American Buddhist monk Bikkhu Bodhi explains the process this way:

"The mind is deliberately kept at the level of *bare attention*, a detached observation of what is happening within us and around us in the present moment. In the practice of right mindfulness, the mind is trained to remain in the present, open, quiet, and alert, contemplating the present event. All judgments and interpretations have to be suspended, or if they occur, just registered and then dropped."

If you want to try a taste of meditation, here are some simple instructions.

BEGINNING TO MEDITATE

Sit quietly on a cushion on the floor, or on a chair, so you are comfortable. Try to align your body so that your back is straight with your vertebrae stacked directly, one on top of the other, and your head is balanced evenly on your torso. This will make it easier for you to remain still without moving.

Focus on your breath as it enters through your nostrils, fills your lungs, and leaves again. Do not control your breath in any way, but simply observe it. You might note, for example, that the air feels cool breathing in and warm breathing out.

Count each exhalation until you get to ten. Then begin again. If you find yourself counting beyond ten, just note that, and return to one again. If thoughts arise in your mind, simply observe them as if they were fluffy clouds crossing a blue sky and let them pass away.

If you are able to pay attention to your breath and not get caught up in attempting to solve your problems or plan your agenda, you have experienced meditation. Perhaps while you are sitting you become aware of feelings that have been suppressed or overlooked during the day. You may even become aware that you are angry with someone, or that you were rattling around all day in a state of annoyance, complaining, because something is bothering you. A thought may arise about what's wrong. Let it pass for the moment, to be examined later when you arise from your cushion. This is meditation.

....

Off the cushion, you can apply the same basic principle in daily life. Sunryu Suzuki writes, "Just to see, and to be ready to see things with our whole mind is *zazen* practice." "Seeing," in this sense of course, is not just seeing. It includes hearing, smelling, touching—the use of all our faculties—in directly apprehending our experience. It is from this state of consciousness that we can experience the world as it really is, as opposed to what we *think* it is.

Mindfulness is connected to the heart, with warmth, with kindness, says Layla Smith, a Zen priest in Larkspur, California:

"What does it feel like in the body, in the heart? We don't try to change the feeling. Mindfulness is not a goal, just a clear comprehension of what is present. And yet there is fruit—just noticing various states, there will naturally arise some detachment and a greater calm, a groundedness in the present, an appreciation of the present."

As human beings with the power of choice, we have the ability to abandon our habits, beliefs, and judgments. We don't need to force ourselves to do this. Simply noting without judgment when we are angry—pausing to observe when we have made a hostile remark, slandered someone, or made a loved one unhappy by once again arriving late—can be the beginning of unraveling our self-defeating behaviors. Greater awareness can reduce the amount of anger in our lives, which in turn frees us to notice more dispassionately what is happening to us and enables the possibility of change. Awareness alone may even cause some of it to fall away.

CHAPTER 6

Pride, Honor, and Other Buttons
OUR SORE SPOTS

T*he Zen Master Hakuin was praised for living a pure life. The village honored him with food and alms. One day, a beautiful girl's parents discovered that she was pregnant. She stubbornly refused to name the father. After continued pressure, she named Hakuin. When the parents confronted Hakuin with the accusation, all he would say was, "Is that so?"*

The parents said, "If you don't deny it, we will have to believe it."

Hakuin replied, "Is that so?"

In a short time, Hakuin had lost his reputation. When the baby was born, it was delivered to him for care. To make a living for himself and the baby, he worked at cleaning rice paddies. After a year, the young lady could not stand it any longer and confessed who the true father was. The parents ran to Hakuin and begged his forgiveness saying, "We now know that you were not the father."

Hakuin replied, "Is that so?"

✦

You see a person at the side of the road changing a tire and having a hard time of it. You say, "Need some help?" The struggling tire changer turns around and blasts you with something like, "Mind your own business!"

What just happened? You pushed a button. You entered into the personal drama taking place in the tire changer's mind. Perhaps his father always told him he was helpless and that he couldn't punch his way out of a paper bag. Because of his painful past experiences, your offer of help is interpreted as an insult.

We're all familiar with the phrase "pushing my buttons," and we all have buttons. The expression captures the notion of an automatic response, unmediated by any thought processes, ready to erupt at the moment one of the demands we make on the world is violated. Pushing one of our buttons produces a fixed, machinelike response, as if we were robots. A computer geek might call it a "macro." Our buttons have been programmed at different times and places and under varying conditions. But our responses are predictably angry and almost certainly pernicious.

"Each of us has 'buttons'—areas where we are sensitive," writes Thubten Chödron in *Working with Anger*. "When our buttons are pushed, we fly off the handle, blaming the other person for upsetting us. But our being upset is a dependently arising process. We contribute the buttons and the other person does the pushing. If we didn't have the buttons, others couldn't push them."

The notion of "pushing my buttons" also implies a pusher. People who know us well, or those who are shrewd enough to intuit our sensitivities, might want to manipulate us by making the very remark or performing the precise action that they know will elicit our fury or discomfort. This leaves us vulnerable and gives others the power to bring unhappiness into our lives.

We may assume that we are innocent in this situation, but in the Buddhist view, we are responsible for our buttons. "As long as we have them, someone will push them," says Chödron, "especially since they are big, red, and flashing . . . Although many times people have no intention of harming us, our buttons get pushed just because they are so sensitive." John Daido Loori, the late abbot of Zen

Mountain Monastery in New York, writes: "One of the things that you realize when you see the nature of the self is that what you do and what happens to you are the same thing. Realizing that you do not exist separately from everything else, you realize responsibility: You are responsible for everything you experience. You can no longer say, 'He made me angry.' How could he make you angry? Only you can make you angry."

Although some things, like lying or cheating or betraying a vow, might be legitimate reasons to take offense, what we're talking about here are the more disproportionate or irrational reactions that have their roots in clinging to our prejudices and past history, or in the Buddhist sense, in "our attachments." We may be attached to independence, like the man changing the tire. Or, if we always get angry when we are criticized, we may be attached to approval.

The story at the beginning of this chapter illustrates what life without buttons looks like. Like most Zen parables, this one takes an extreme position to make its points. The first lesson is that Hakuin was not attached to his reputation to the extent of caring what other people thought of him. (No button.) The fact that they changed their opinion did not alter his self-esteem. He was willing to accept what life brought him and experiment with it. Perhaps he would enjoy being a father.

The second lesson is that what other people think of you is irrelevant if you are secure in who you are. Hakuin was no more impressed with the apology than he was with the false accusation. Most people who read this parable for the first time are puzzled that Hakuin would not defend himself. They cannot conceive of not responding to a false accusation. Behind this bewilderment lie our usual definitions of pride and honor and our insecurity about them.

To remove this unnecessary source of anger from our lives we must recognize our own buttons. A typical button panel might involve the following issues:

Can you identify the things that always get your goat? Naming your buttons and the demands underlying them can go a long way to deactivating them. Take a moment to be aware of situations in your life that automatically trigger anger.

You might start with, "I can't stand it whenever . . ." or, "It really bugs me when . . ."

Some possibilities include:

I hate being criticized. (approval)

I hate it when somebody thinks he is better than I am. (pride)

I hate to be ordered around or told what to do. (independence)

I can't stand it when someone talks back or argues with me. (respect)

I don't like it when a friend doesn't trust me. (honor)

I go ape when my girlfriend is friendly with other guys. (jealousy)

✦ *Exercise* WHAT ARE YOUR BUTTONS?

Remember to differentiate between a complaint, which puts the onus on the other person, and a "button," which reveals a particular sensitivity and promotes further exploration. List as many of your buttons as you can here.

_____

_____

_____

_____

_____

The names we give our buttons are sometimes warped versions of their original meaning. The desire for honor or to avoid criticism may have value. But the word "honor" as a description of a desirable personality trait is so often misused that it seldom retains its pure meaning. Almost invariably, when someone perceives his or her "honor" to have been violated, the response is destructive. The "honor" killings committed in some societies, for instance, have more to do with maintaining male-role power, control, and superiority than with honesty and integrity. In such societies, a woman who has been raped may be ostracized or stoned by her family because their "honor" has been violated.

But such reactions are not restricted to other cultures. In our society, defending one's "honor" has led to homicide. In an article about juvenile crime in New York, one young man was asked why he shot someone. His answer was, "He dissed my girlfriend. What else could I do?"

Our pride button may be pushed when we are overly attached to the opinion of others, which may be irrelevant to our intrinsic worth. Buddhism takes the view that it's foolish to take the opinions of the outside world, which may fluctuate daily if not from moment to moment, as any serious measure of ourselves. As His Holiness, the Dalai Lama, once famously said of himself: "One day Nobel Prize, next day pile of shit!"

Possessiveness, unlike pride and honor, is a problem under any definition. When jealousy occurs in a love relationship, it may well be more a measure of how insecure you are than how much you love the other person, and anger is not the appropriate response.

In general, our buttons were programmed at some time long ago in the past. The conditions under which these particular sensitivities arose may no longer be relevant, and our past responses even less so. We are not still the insecure, helpless person we once were, and today we have more effective ways of dealing with the things that once set us off than to engage in an impotent expression of anger.

Our automatic responses—especially to something perceived as criticism—may cut us off from learning useful things about ourselves. Even if the criticism is justified, our anger response doesn't allow us to hear it. I have often marveled at variations of the following dialogue:

1st Person: "Wow, was I dumb to do that."

2nd Person: "You sure were."

1st Person (now angry): "Are you calling me dumb?"

When anger is provoked by one of our buttons being pushed, we need to be willing to look constructively at what caused it. Criticism is often unwelcome for various reasons, but if we immediately go on the defensive, we can't distinguish between valid, helpful criticism and unfair criticism. If you have an insecurity button that gets pushed when you are criticized, try to quell the automatic internal storm that erupts: "Who is she to criticize me?" "He thinks he knows better than I do." "If I don't respond strongly, she'll think I'm admitting fault." This reaction short-circuits the process of seeing whether the criticism has value and correcting the underlying problem.

Letting our buttons be pushed deprives us of the opportunity to learn and perhaps improve our relationship with the person offering the criticism. If instead of raising your shield, you listen and say, "Thank you. I'll think about what you said," there may be an opportunity to improve your performance as well as to deepen your relationship. If a person takes the risk of criticizing you—and possibly incurring your wrath—it may be because she cares enough about you and your relationship to do so. Behind the comment there's often an implicit assumption that you can and will do better next time.

✦

Now that you've identified your buttons, you may be able to notice the next time one is being pushed and be able to pause before your habitual reaction. If you recognize that you have an automatic response to being criticized or insulted, it may open the way to a more constructive or effective response.

✦ DEACTIVATING OUR BUTTONS

Take a look at the list you made of your buttons (pages 93–94). For each item, think about the original circumstances under which your sensitivity to the issue arose. Are you still that person? Do you still need to respond angrily if someone pushes that button? What purpose would your anger serve? What problems would it cause for you? Might not the reaction, "Is that so?" serve you better?

Anger and Hatred

One way some people deal with things that trigger their anger is to mark entire areas off-limits. When our aversions become fixed, they become hatreds. Hate is ossified anger. We may declare that we hate a particular group of people and therefore won't deal with them. Those persons are "off-limits" to us. These may be common prejudices against people whom some consider to be inferior—fat people, Jews, African Americans, homosexuals.

Hate is pernicious, and when we carry it within us, it causes damage. The Buddha said:

> *Hate brings great misfortune,*
> *Hate churns up and harms the mind.*
> *This fearful danger deep within*
> *Most people do not understand.*

In recent years, we've witnessed outpourings of anger and hate on both sides of the political spectrum. But as one blogger commented in *The New York Times*, "eight years of hate-filled liberal blogs and cartoons about Bush improved his performance no more than conservative hate-filled blogs and cartoons improved Clinton's." And, unfortunately, the hatred of one side fuels the hatred of the other.

In politics, a passionate commitment to one set of beliefs or another may have a rational basis. But in other cases, the notion that someone has offended us may simply be a function of projecting our ideologies onto the outside world by "mind reading." A fervent feminist may feel disrespected when a man opens a door for her or pauses to let her enter an elevator first. I once witnessed a woman stand her ground and insist that an elderly man precede her. When she got off the elevator, he turned to me and said: "I hate it when people do things like that just because I'm old."

When we hate, it can make us oblivious to changes since our prejudice was formed. A woman attorney represented a client who had been sued over a failed business deal. When he came in with the summons, he handed the papers to her and said, "It's bad enough getting sued, but the attorney on the other side is a woman. I hate women attorneys." My friend cleared her throat. Her client quickly said, "Present company excepted."

By acting out our prejudices we also cut ourselves off from the richness our world has to offer. With its policy of anti-Semitism, Nazi Germany denied itself the use of the resources of its entire Jewish population. "Our German scientists were better than their German scientists" was the pithy summary of the war's outcome by one of Churchill's closest aides. Likewise, the Spanish Inquisition expelled the Muslims whose scientific and cultural contributions had created the most advanced civilization in Europe at the time.

In far lesser ways, we limit our lives and resources with each ossified hatred.

From a Buddhist standpoint, we always deprive ourselves of a full enjoyment of life when we recoil from the universe. Robert Thurman, a leading Western authority on Tibetan Buddhism, used the following example to explain this:

"You get on a subway car. Midway to the next station, it stops. Somehow you know that it will never start again and you will spend the rest of your life here. At that point, you figure you better help the drunk who is puking on himself, console the person who appears to be crazy, and get to know the teenage punk who scares the hell out of you."

Anger may occasionally dissolve into humor or even affection on the spot, but when we harbor hate, changing our attitude is far more difficult. Among older Jews, there is a saying, "Scratch a gentile and find an anti-Semite." Based on centuries of pain, this is an apprehension that anti-Semitism may be pervasive even if it is not expressed openly. But it may also be a refusal to recognize that profound changes have taken place in our society. Thus, prejudice is reciprocated and inhibits further dialogue and improved relationships.

Pushing Other People's Buttons

When we become aware of our own buttons, we also become more aware that other people have sensitivities that cause them to react irrationally. In some cases, we may make what we think is an innocent remark that sets someone off. We often acknowledge this by saying, "Oops, I guess I touched a nerve." But in other situations, we may not be so innocent. We may be vaguely aware that a given remark is offensive, but say it anyway to express our own annoyance. And sometimes, we may deliberately push another's buttons as an outright provocation.

Becoming aware of other people's buttons and refraining from pushing them is one of the ways in which we become more compassionate. And by taking responsibility for recognizing our own buttons and deactivating them, we reduce the amount of anger circulating out there in the world.

CHAPTER 7

Giving and Receiving
SHIFTING THE EMOTIONAL BALANCE

Generosity, kind words,
Doing a good turn for others,
And treating all people alike:
These bonds of sympathy are to the world
What the linchpin is to the wheel.

—The Buddha

For it is in giving that we receive.

—St. Francis of Assisi

Giving and receiving freely and graciously is a way to improve our lives and the world around us. Generosity and courtesy are social lubricants that reduce the friction of social interaction. When people are courteous in traffic, allowing others to pull in ahead of them and so forth, not only does traffic move more smoothly, but those who are on the receiving end of such small favors find their lives easier and happier, an attitude they are more likely to pass on to others they encounter during the day. To adopt giving and receiving as a way of life, without fear of being taken advantage of or seeking favor, can go a long way to releasing us from anger. Even if these gifts are small, like going out of our way to compliment someone on service or allowing someone to enter a crowded traffic lane, or expressing affection or gratitude instead of assuming someone knows how we feel, the effect is to spread goodwill, just as rude and inconsiderate behavior spreads anger.

Unfortunately, many of us see ourselves as the lone quarterback carrying the ball and running down the field with the guys on the other team doing their best to tackle us. We may also suspect, at times, that the people on our team who should be protecting or helping us are not fully into that task. Like many of the preconceptions we have about our lives and those with whom we interact, this one is probably more false than true. But it can give rise to a vague, chronic anger and the feeling that we are not getting the support and respect we deserve or our fair share of life's goodies.

Old habits may cause us to imagine a world that is hostile to us. Once when I was hiking, I saw a lovely little canyon beyond a gate. I wanted to explore it, but saw a sign on the gate and, although it was too far away to read, I assumed it said, "Keep Out." Later, when I went back, I saw that what it actually said was, "Please close the gate after entering." Likewise, our lack of awareness may convert a wall or a hole in the ground into a dangerous obstacle. We may be prone to see a hose in the garden as not only a snake but a poisonous one. Past experiences may cause us to react inappropriately to new circumstances. If you stopped to help someone at the side of the road and were rudely spurned, does that mean that you should never help anyone again? The reality is that when we meet the world directly without the intervention of our past "bank" of experience, we generally find it to be more helpful and loving than we expected.

One of the ways that we shut out help is that we are under the illusion that we exist separately and independently from others. In his book *The Light Inside the Dark*, John Tarrant tells the story of a friend who was sailing on the San Francisco Bay when he had a sharp, sudden pain that disabled him. What followed was a series of helping hands— his friends who sailed the boat, the coast guard who took him to shore, the ambulance driver, and the doctor who saved his life. He said:

I have always relied on myself. I have tried to help
others, but have done things alone and it has always
worked, more or less. But here I could not rely
on myself. I fell through the bottom, and hands
reached out to catch me. Of all the events around
my illness, that is the most shocking. That is what
asks for the greatest change in how I see the world.

Some of us may have had similar experiences when
traveling in a country where we don't speak the language.
Deprived of our usual coping mechanisms and forced to
rely on others, we may find that the world takes us in. A
Canadian couple was driving through the Egyptian desert
when their off-road vehicle got stuck in the sand. Before
they had time to panic, a group of villagers, carrying a tray
with food and drink, appeared out of nowhere to help the
couple dig out and get on their way. Egypt is a country with
a particularly strong tradition of hospitality, but similar
stories from throughout the world are common.

"The fundamental delusion of human beings is the
belief that we exist separately and independently from
the rest of the universe," writes former San Francisco Zen
Center abbot Reb Anderson in *Being Upright*. "There is the
whole universe, a human thinks, plus something—and that
something is me." But the cardinal doctrine in Buddhism

is that all things in the universe are deeply connected and that they mutually create one another; therefore they have no inherent, independent existence. The Buddha called this *pratitya samutpada*, which is translated variously as "dependent co-arising" or "interdependent arising." Nothing in the universe arises or exists independently; everything is interconnected in an incredibly complex web of cause and effect.

In our individual striving for personal success, we often forget the many people who helped us along the way with a word of encouragement, an idea, or a suggestion whose source we soon forget and think of as our own. The collaboration in movies that is often recognized in interminable thank-you's at the Academy Awards exists in all our lives in perhaps less obvious ways. It is not all-powerful You who has single-handedly and by sheer force of individual will and genius wrested victory from the world, but the cooperation and culmination of many forces and efforts.

The scientific concept of the Butterfly Effect in chaos theory—that the smallest initial action can have a far-reaching ripple effect, so that a butterfly's wings flapping in Beijing may ultimately affect the weather in New York—captures part of the Buddhist idea of interdependence. But think of the Butterfly Effect multiplied a zillion times and affecting not only physical actions but interpersonal ones as well. Buddhism uses the metaphor of Indra's net to express how everything in the universe influences and reflects back on everything else in an infinite number of concatenations. In the heavenly abode of the god Indra, a wonderful net stretches out infinitely in all directions. A single glittering jewel hangs in each "eye" of the net, and on the faceted surface of each jewel is reflected every other jewel in the net, each of which also reflects all the others.

Generosity and Keeping Score

Just as we experience anger when we feel our demands haven't been met, so our failure to meet the requests of others may engender anger in them and lead to a cycle of animosity. Our refusal to meet unreasonable demands is justified and understandable. For instance, if someone asks us to help them do something unethical, we have not only a right, but a responsibility to refuse. However, even though a request is reasonable and we have the ability to meet it, we may choose not to. We may decide that our books are out of balance, that we've given more than we're receiving. "I am always doing things for him, and he never does anything for me." Or we may play the martyr with phrases like, "Nobody really appreciates what I do for them."

Keeping score creates resentment, which is a way of feeding chronic low-level anger.

Some people may habitually say no to any suggestion or request because they think they're being asked for more than they want to give. Or they may believe that if they say yes, they'll be descending the slippery slope of "give an inch and they'll take a foot . . . or a mile." Others may fear that saying yes will lead to a loss of control. On her retirement from a New York City welfare agency, a woman was asked by *The New York Times* what thirty years of service had taught her. She replied that she had learned to always say no to a request. Her reason was that if you say no, you can always change it to yes later, but that it was difficult to do the opposite. Although this tactic may occasionally have some value in a bureaucracy, if practiced in everyday life, it is likely to shrivel our intimate relationships and alienate us from the neighbors, friends, and business associates on whom we depend.

Sometimes, we may hesitate to meet other people's needs because we don't know how our efforts will be received. When Doris, who belonged to a closely-knit group of docents at a local museum, came down with terminal cancer and had less than a year to live, everyone wanted to do something for her. But when the group talked about how to help, every suggestion turned into a "yes, but."

"Well, we could offer to go and sit with her."

"Yes, but maybe she doesn't want company."

"We could take meals to her."

"Yes, but she might think we see her as an invalid."

"We could send a gift basket."

"Yes, but that might not really be what she needs."

When word of this quandary got back to Doris, she sat down and made a list of things people might do for her and sent it to several of her docent friends.

The list was passed around and each person gladly signed up for one or more tasks. Doris had lifted the vague sense of guilt and the frustration they'd felt by not knowing what to do for her. Everyone felt she had given *them* a gift. In fact, she had. She had expressed what they could not know, which was what she really needed and desired.

Another reason that we may not willingly meet other people's requests is the belief that being generous may invite people to take advantage of us. We may think that our generosity goes unnoticed or unrewarded. There is even a popular saying that "No good deed goes unpunished." The greater truth is "What goes around, comes around." What you project is what you get back.

"Have you ever known a generous person who was unhappy?" asked the Buddhist sage Shantideva. It is almost impossible to be generous without creating goodwill, not only in those to whom we give, but also in those who observe our generous nature. The illusion that generous people are taken advantage of is not validated in practice. "The world is good-natured to people who are good-natured," wrote William Makepeace Thackeray. Those who operate out of a sense of fullness rather than scarcity find their lives enriched in many ways. We can confirm this by experimenting with small acts of generosity or "random acts of kindness" and then observing the results of these acts.

In a popular workshop game called Econcom, the group is divided into several teams. Each team receives various resources. The object is to see which team, by buying and trading resources, can acquire the most wealth. Econcom was designed so that the participants eventually discover that the cooperative use of resources produces the greatest wealth for all. Many experiments have replicated the same phenomenon; cooperation consistently produces the best outcome.

Generosity is a reasoned act of kindness and not a show of wealth. Nor should giving a beggar an occasional dollar serve as an excuse for not being involved with social justice. The injustice that exists in the world is not just other people's misfortune, but inevitably has something to do with institutions and economic structures in which we all have a part. And it may just be the luck of the draw that

yours is the occupation that is suddenly obsolete, or your
company that's moved out of town and left you jobless and
impoverished. To paraphrase the Dalai Lama, "One day
CEO, next day bag of shit."

✦ *Exercise* RANDOM ACTS OF KINDNESS

It's highly likely that you have been the recipient of at least
a small act of kindness recently. Can you list one or more?
Did you acknowledge the gift, or thank the person who gave
it to you? Do you feel differently after giving a gift than you
do after receiving one?

The idea of the exercise above is not to keep score. It is to
be aware of how you feel when making or receiving a gift. This
causes you to feel more kinship with other people. Cultivating
small moments of pleasure and happiness will fortify you

to withstand the irritations and annoyances that lead to anger. "Constantly note anything that is pleasing," says Pema Chödrön. "Tiny things, little things. You were cold, and you put on your coat, and now you feel warm. Throughout the day, you feel a multitude of moments of fleeting happiness. You become more easily touched, more grateful for the smallest things." This "cheerfulness practice," as Chödrön calls it, shifts the balance in your emotional life and makes it easier to deal with hard things.

OFFERING AND RECEIVING GIFTS

During the day, be aware of opportunities to give a small gift. Hold the door open for the person entering behind you. Say "yes" when someone asks you to go to the movie he prefers rather than the one you have in mind. Give credit at work to an assistant or co-worker who's contributed to the success of your project. Share your lunch with a co-worker who is looking enviously at the repast that your significant other has prepared.

Note to yourself: "I have just given a gift" and be aware of how you feel. More important than the appreciation you may receive back is the cultivation in yourself of compassion and generosity.

Likewise, become more aware of those moments when someone has gone out of their way for you, or given you something. Your husband makes a special effort to prepare your favorite dish. Your wife offers to take the car in for servicing so you can get a free afternoon. A friend, who knows you've suffered some misfortune, calls to find out how you are. Someone honors your preference over her own.

You may or may not have the chance to say "thank you," but say to yourself, "I have just received a gift."

The Giver Should Be Thankful

While Seisetsu was the master of the temple of Engaku in Japan he needed larger quarters, because those in which he was teaching were overcrowded. The local merchant Umezu Seibei decided to donate five hundred pieces of gold called ryo toward the construction of a more commodious school. He brought this money to the teacher.

Seisetsu said: "All right, I will take it."

Umezu gave Seisetsu the sack of gold, but he was dissatisfied with the attitude of the teacher. One might live a whole year on three ryo, and the merchant had not even been thanked for five hundred.

"In that sack are five hundred ryo," hinted Umezu.

"You told me that before," replied Seisetsu.

"Even if I am a wealthy merchant, five hundred ryo is a lot of money," said Umezu.

"Do you want me to thank you for it?" asked Seisetsu.

"You ought to," replied Umezu.

"Why should I?" inquired Seisetsu. "The giver should be thankful."

✦

Like many Zen parables, this one initially seems impenetrable. But viewed from the Buddhist perspective of the interconnectedness of all things, it becomes more intelligible. In his book *Vedanta: Seven Steps to Samadhi*, the spiritual leader Osho says, "On the temple it is written even still . . . that the giver should be thankful; only then is it a sharing. . . . Somebody accepted you through your gift. He could have rejected [it], there was no necessity to accept it. The giver should be thankful. Then it becomes a sharing, otherwise it is always a bargain. You are expecting something—something more valuable than you have given. When someone becomes enlightened, he can share, and he will do whatsoever he can just to share it."

Laura Cade, a Washington member of Milkin' Mamas Breast Milk Bank, makes an eloquent comment on this parable. When her son was a newborn she read about breast milk donation. "The idea of giving this magical substance to babies who really need it pulled on my heartstrings, but I simply didn't have the energy then." But later, when she was able to give, she said, "All the feeling of compassion and warmth I had felt toward the babies I'd be giving my

milk to came back full force. . . . I was reminded of an old
Zen parable that's called 'The Giver Should Be Thankful,'
for I have never given a gift that comes close to the level
of thankfulness I feel for the privilege of being a breast
milk donor."

Just as many people find it easier to fulfill a request
than to voice one, some people find it easier to give
than to receive. But in receiving graciously, in accepting
wholeheartedly, we are also giving. We are allowing the
giver to enter into relationship with us, acknowledging
his good will, and sharing in our common humanity and
interdependence. In *Zen Mind, Beginner's Mind*, Shunryu
Suzuki writes, "Everything is originally one, the big 'I.'
It is impossible to distinguish what is giving and what is
receiving."And Dogen, the thirteenth-century founder of the
Soto school of Zen, says, "In becoming a giver or a receiver,
we establish an affinity with all creatures in the world."

We cannot know all the implications and ultimate
results of our actions. But just as a stone thrown into a
lake sends ripples to far shores, and a butterfly's wings stir
currents throughout the atmosphere, so our interactions
with other beings send reverberations out into the universe.

CHAPTER 8

The Mythology of Happiness

DO WE REALLY KNOW WHAT'S GOOD FOR US?

A landlord came to the Zen master in a state of distress. One of his stable hands had left the door to the barn open and his prize stallion had escaped. "What a disaster!" the man cried. The master replied only, "I don't know." The landlord left in disgust.

A few days later, the stallion returned to the barn followed by three wild mares. The landlord returned to the master and said, "It wasn't a disaster. It was a blessing." The master replied, "I don't know." The landlord left, doubting the wisdom of the master.

When the landlord's son was breaking the mares, he was thrown and broke his leg. The landlord returned to the master and told him of the event and said the master was right that it was not a blessing. The master replied, "I don't know."

When the soldiers of the emperor came to recruit young men for an upcoming battle, they left the son behind because of his broken leg. The son said, "Father, what a blessing my broken leg is." The father said, "I don't know."

✦

John Tarrant has characterized Buddhism as "the technology of happiness." By this he means that it is a system or method to help liberate us from suffering by enabling us to see things as they are and not as we have been conditioned to think they are. What I call our "mythology of happiness" is the conditioning that may have us believe that things like fame, money, or power will make us happy and that also seduces us to believe in the quick and transient fix.

We believe that we know what makes us happy and what is in our best interest, only to have life inform us differently. When our goals and expectations are not met, we often become frustrated and angry. When I asked my Buddhist teacher, Patrick Hawk, a Zen master as well as a Catholic priest, why anger persists, he gave me the sort of answer that a Zen master is so good at. It seems cryptic at first but goes off like slow-motion fireworks in your mind. He said one cause of the persistence of anger is that we insist that our lives have meaning. On the surface, the search for a meaningful life might sound exemplary but, he continued, the problem arises when we insist that it be *the meaning we choose.* "The human brain is a successful meaning machine," he says. "We make sense of our world by creating meaning, but by doing so we also filter out a great deal of the world. According to Buddhism, there is no inherent meaning in anything. Everything just is—just as it is." By choosing certain goals or charting a particular meaning or course for our lives, we arbitrarily shut out many of the options open to us. Then when the universe does not bow to our will and fulfill the goal or meaning we have chosen, that causes disappointment and can leave us feeling perpetually angry.

On the simpler, more obvious level illustrated by the opening parable, the day-to-day or even minute-by-minute events that make us angry when our momentary desires are thwarted may turn out to be for the best. By the same token, getting what we think we want may have unintended consequences that are ultimately unfortunate. As the parable illustrates, the law of the universe is change. The Buddhist ideal of non-attachment—treating the things that occur in our lives with a certain detachment, which is sometimes summarized as "no desire, no aversion" or "keeping the mind of 'don't know'"—was developed as an antidote to protect us from unnecessary suffering amid the constant loss and change that is characteristic of human life.

A woman I know fell in love for the first time when she was twenty-five years old. The object of her affections was a rather paternalistic man who made many decisions for her and seemed to her at the time the epitome of the good father. She was sure that marrying him would be the best thing that could happen to her. When he left her for another woman, she was devastated and for a long time cherished the idea that if only they had married her life would have been blissfully happy. Years later, she encountered him again. The qualities that had initially attracted her had disappeared. His lack of fidelity to his wife had caused her to leave him and he referred to his two sons as "the little jerks." She could only thank her lucky stars that he had rejected her.

✦ *Exercise* UNINTENDED CONSEQUENCES

Can you recall an instance in your life when something happened that you considered an absolute disaster and tried to avoid at all cost, but later worked out for the better?

✎

_____

_____

_____

_____

✦ Can you recall instances when the opposite happened,
when a greatly anticipated event turned out to be a disaster?

✎

_____

_____

_____

_____

The fact that we think we know what will make us
happy leaves us pursuing our "mythology of happiness"
rather than being content with where we are right now and
perhaps overlooking opportunities for joy standing beside
our path. To achieve real contentment, we need to examine
the hodgepodge of conditioning created by our parents, the

advertising industry, and other forces that go into fabricating our myth. This conditioning may have arisen from good, or perhaps not so good, intentions. When you were a child and fell down, your mother may have offered you a cookie, saying something like, "Eat this, and you'll feel better." To the extent that this became part of your mythology of happiness, it may have led to obesity, or to emotional or physical ills.

The advertising industry spends millions of dollars creating mythologies. Tobacco companies went to great lengths to suggest that there is something not only satisfying but healthy and sexy about smoking, while manufacturing cigarettes that were both harmful and highly addictive. Hollywood has sold the notion that a handsome husband, a beautiful wife, or a fast car is the royal road to happiness. In general, our culture inculcates the expectation that fame, money, power, and possessions are a guarantee of satisfaction, even in the face of so much evidence in the lives of the rich and powerful to the contrary.

The classic case of the failure of the myth of happiness is the million-dollar lottery winner. For various reasons, 90 percent of lottery winners say five years later that they wish they hadn't won. To begin with, after taxes and inflation, one actually gets about one quarter of this amount, or about $50,000 each year for twenty years. Then there are the relatives the winner hasn't seen in years suddenly appearing on the doorstep asking for help, the new "friends" trying to get a piece of the action, and all the problems of managing the newfound money.

Sex is another powerful myth that our society glamorizes—so much so that many believe that satisfying this desire is a precondition to happiness. In other words, if I am not sleeping with someone on a regular basis, then I cannot be happy. An acquaintance, who is generally dissatisfied with his lot, reported that he had unexpectedly gotten laid, and, as a result, was now happy. I didn't bother to ask how long his contentment would last because I knew him well enough to know that it would be no longer than it takes to replenish the testosterone.

A Buddhist sutra captures the reality of such transient pleasure:

> *If one, longing for sensual pleasure, achieves it,*
> *Yes, he's enraptured at heart.*
> *The mortal gets what he wants.*
> *But when for that person—longing, desiring—*
> *   the pleasures diminish,*
> *He's shattered, as if shot with an arrow.*

This doesn't mean that Buddhism is down on either sex or pleasure. When the sutras refer to letting go of "desire," they are not saying that you cannot enjoy sensual pleasure. The relevant Buddhist precept is generally stated as, "A disciple of Buddha does not misuse sexuality." That would condemn forced sex and the kind of compulsive sexual expression that might be considered an addiction.

The desire that is pernicious from the Buddhist perspective is clinging to things that are transient. "When you see through the illusion of the permanent self or the persistence of material things, then you're free," says Patrick Hawk. "The idea is not to be caught in any one stance or dependence."

Another problem with desire is that many of the things we yearn for do not satisfy us when we get them. In a 2003 study at Harvard, students were asked whether they would prefer (a) $50,000 a year, while others got half that, or (b) $100,000, while others got twice as much. A majority chose (a). They were happy with less, as long as they were better off than others. Other studies have confirmed this phenomenon. Pleasure at your own pay raise can vanish when you learn that a co-worker has been given a larger one.

When we are anxious, we may go shopping whether we can afford to or not. If we can't afford the things we buy, the resulting debt becomes an additional source of anxiety. And even if we can afford them, we may find that, as a Zen proverb teaches, "Possessions we intend to possess, end up possessing us."

A Western version of this, with a bit of irony thrown in, says: "The two happiest days in a boat owner's life are the day he buys a boat and the day he sells it."

Our mythology of happiness is not limited to material things. The things we believe will make us happy may be tangible, intangible, or even spiritual. My childhood friend Jim was a jock as a kid; he was a gymnast and also played many other sports. He attended a good college, and despite some learning disabilities, soldiered on to a Ph.D. because his overbearing father thought that becoming a college professor was the epitome of success. Jim succeeded in getting an appointment at a state college but found that he hated academia. Once when someone asked him how things were at work, I watched a film of sweat cover his arms. He told me at the time that he would be much happier if he were working at the YMCA teaching kids sports or how to work out.

Andre Agassi, who I would have thought had it all, revealed on *60 Minutes* that he never liked playing tennis, and that it made him miserable. This, despite being rated the number one tennis player in the world!

✦ *Exercise* WHAT IS YOUR MYTHOLOGY?

The things that you believe will make you happy are not necessarily wrong for you. The goal here is simply to be aware of them and to see how they affect your life.

List those things you think will make you happy.
Possibilities might include Fame, Beauty, Wealth, Popularity,
A Prestige Profession, Achievement, Marrying Up, Spirituality.

Now comment on: which ones you have achieved; how each
has contributed to your happiness; and what has been the
price of that happiness.

The mythology of happiness is also found in one's Negative Rules. Some examples of these rules are:

• If I get too close to someone, I will end up being hurt.

• If I let my emotions show, people will perceive me as vulnerable and take advantage of me.

• If I don't get angry, the person who's offended me will think I'm a coward or that I approve of what he did.

• If I am generous, people will use me.

✦ *Exercise* WHAT ARE YOUR NEGATIVE RULES?

_____

_____

_____

_____

_____

_____

_____

_____

Are there some of those negative rules that, if abandoned, might lead the way to greater happiness?

If we satisfy the needs created by our mythology and still are not happy or experience only transient satisfaction, the result is likely to be anger. This anger may not be conscious and clearly defined but simply felt as an ongoing demand that we get another pleasure fix. We further compound the problem if we believe, probably mistakenly, that our friends who got the same fix—the car or the boat—are happy while we are not.

De-Mythification

Liberating ourselves from our mythology is a challenging task because it's so deeply rooted in our conditioning. Some of us are so heavily invested in our habitual ways that we have come to believe that, for instance, making money defines who we are. We may persist in this pursuit even though there are signs that it is interfering with our happiness. Someone whose need to make money is so all-consuming may neglect his family and everything else. Yet giving up his belief might be seen as a "death" or loss of identity. This kind of death is referred to in Zen as "the small death" and is considered a spiritual gain.

Put another way, we refuse to take the risk of changing jobs or relationships or to control our eating because we cling to these things when we are emotionally upset. By being unwilling to disturb the habitual order of our lives or to endure emotional pain, we allow ourselves to stay stuck in a situation where our demands are not met on an ongoing basis. A general dissatisfaction with our lives can be the result.

The fact that we think we know what will make us happy leaves us with a closed mind, pursuing our mythology rather than being content with where we are right now. As we said at the beginning, Buddhism provides a methodology for happiness. Its method of deconditioning is performed by meditation: "Turning the mind back to look at itself," as Buddhist sage Dogen described it. When we meditate, we can become a silent observer of our thoughts and beliefs. We can then look detachedly at what we are doing that impairs our happiness and, conversely, what engenders it. (See Beginning to Meditate on page 85.)

Ultimately, our goals can be like the possessions that end up possessing us. The solution is to recognize that they exist only by our own creation. "Realize that it is we who are giving them meaning," says Patrick Hawk. If your goals don't work out, change them. Be flexible. Leave yourself open to other possibilities. "When you see through the illusion of meaning, then you are truly free."

Abandoning our fantasies of what will bring us happiness will result in less anger by eliminating a range of dissatisfactions and frustrations that result from them. Understanding that we do not know how an event will turn out allows us to live in the present moment without preconceptions of what is good for us. It frees us to experiment with our lives and increases the odds of finding happiness. The true treasure is equanimity and, in the midst of the apparent joys and disasters of life, keeping the mind of "don't know."

CHAPTER 9

Unshakeable Calm
DEALING WITH
THE ANGER OF OTHERS

*O*nce *when the Buddha was teaching near the city of Rajagaha, a Brahman learned that one of his clan had left his home and become a monk under the Blessed One. The Brahman was angry and displeased and went to see the Buddha. When he arrived, he reviled and abused him in rude and harsh speech.*

Thus being spoken to, the Blessed One said: "How is it, Brahman: Do you sometimes receive visits from friends, relatives or other guests?"

"Yes, Master Gotama, I sometimes have visitors."

"When they come, do you offer them various kinds of foods and a place for resting?"

"Yes, I sometimes do so."

"But if, Brahman, your visitors do not accept what you offer, to whom does it then belong?"

"Well, Master Gotama, if they do not accept it, these things remain with us."

"It is just so in this case, Brahman: you revile us who do not revile in return, you scold us who do not scold in return, you abuse us who do not abuse in return. So we do not accept it from you and hence it remains with you, it belongs to you, Brahman . . ."

✦

No matter how successful we are at learning to deal with our own anger, we live in a world in which we will be subject to the anger of others.

In our society, we learn that if someone has insulted us we *should* be angry in return. Being on the receiving end of someone's anger is a lot like being punched. Our fight-or-flight response gets triggered, our adrenaline kicks in, and we respond from our primitive, nonrational limbic brain. "Nobody gets away with doing that to me!" is our indignant response. We think that the only way to assuage the pain of anger is to trade punches and inflict pain in return. In fact, all that happens is an escalation of anger on both sides.

Nevertheless, various Buddhist masters have used artful ways to respond when anger is directed toward them.

Chögyam Trungpa, one of the first masters to bring Tibetan Buddhism to America, described one possibility this way:

> The practice of patience means not returning threats, anger, attacks or insults. But this does not mean being purely passive. Instead we use the other person's energy, as in judo. . . . Our response is self-defensive in the sense that we do not return such a person's threat, and at the same time we prevent further aggression by allowing the other person's own energy to undercut itself.

Students of judo and other martial arts are taught that if someone is coming at you rapidly, just step aside at the last moment; the aggressor may well fall on his face. But simply not reacting is a kind of judo; you let the anger go by you as if it were a passing breeze. "You allow a lot of space for the other person's energy without judgment and without reaction," explains David Schneider, a senior teacher in Trungpa's Shambhala lineage. "This energy then either wears itself out, or is noticed—heard—by the person. When that happens, often it drops away. The reason that this is not purely passive is that it requires a great deal of energy to allow space, and to not judge and not return anger. It requires strength and insight to hold your seat."

In *An Open Heart*, the Dalai Lama writes, "If we have a positive mental attitude, then even when surrounded by hostility, we shall not lack inner peace." If we return anger with anger, the hostile energy increases exponentially and we lose all equanimity. "Imagine that your neighbor hates you and is always creating problems for you," His Holiness writes. "If you lose your temper and develop hatred toward him, your digestion is harmed, your sound sleep goes and you have to start to use tranquilizers and sleeping pills. . . . Your mood is affected; as a result, your old friends hesitate to visit you. You gradually get more white hair and wrinkles, and you may eventually develop more serious health problems. Then your neighbor is really happy. Without having inflicted any physical harm, he has fulfilled his wish.

"If, in spite of his injustices, you remain calm, happy and peaceful, your health remains strong, you continue to be joyful and more friends come visit you. Your life becomes more successful. This really brings about worry in your neighbor's mind. I think this is the wise way to inflict harm upon your neighbor. I do not mean this as a joke. I have a certain amount of experience here."

The Dalai Lama has had lifelong training in compassion and dealing with his own anger as well as that of others. But the approach Buddhism prescribes is the same for all—not to return anger and escalate aggression. In dealing with the emotion that arises when we are attacked, it's necessary to first allow space for the other person's anger without reacting. Remaining strong and calm can sometimes reveal to our attacker the futility or disproportion of his angry display, but even if not, it enables us to respond reasonably and effectively.

Shosan Victoria Austin, a Soto Zen priest at the San Francisco Zen Center, suggests the following when confronted with anger.

. . . .

DON'T REACT, RESPOND

When confronted with someone else's anger, use these steps.

1. Make space before speaking or responding. Take some deep breaths.

2. Check the face and body of the person in front of you to understand what's going on. Observe physiological cues. Watch especially for changes in the trust level. When a person becomes more relaxed, their eyes will be open and they will lean slightly toward you.

3. Consider the consequences of not doing anything—whether something that might be helpful in the short run may lead to harm later.

4. Ask yourself: What assumptions am I making? Ask the person what the problem is. Consider your involvement in causing it.

5. Respect and empathize with both your own boundaries, values, and limitations and those of the other person.

A conflict may be the result of differing values, for instance, two family members disagreeing about whether to take care of a parent in a nursing facility or at home. One wants safety for her, the other wants her happiness. The safety-minded person might come clean and admit, "I can't be here all the time; I'm afraid she might hurt herself." The other might say, "I would always be upset with myself if I didn't support Mother's wishes." Then it becomes an argument about concerns instead of positions.

6. Speak from right attitude. Ask yourself, "What do I really need to communicate to this person?" and refrain from venting your feelings for other motives. Check for self-indulgence, ill will, potential harm in one's own words and actions. Ask yourself not only *what* must I say, but *how* must I say it.

7. Deliberately, *do not take revenge.* In Buddhism, the basic vow is benefiting all beings, not everyone except this particular person.

—Shosan Victoria Austin

....

Of course there are some instances of anger where we should just let it pass by and not react at all. For example, in a single instance of another's anger, like a moment of road rage, when a driver yells an insult, the best response is not to respond. Because we won't relate to this person again, we are free not to participate in his fight club. (Unfortunately there are far too many members already.) Sure, it would be nice if we could have a nice dispassionate talk with him. But this is not likely to happen, and if it did, there's little chance that it would do any good. For one thing, if you were to talk with the driver, you'd step into his preconceptions—one of which is that you are a total incompetent. For another thing, his anger may not be about you or what you did at all. He may simply have been set to vent his rage. If that's the case, nothing you can say or do will deal with the real source of his anger.

In a casual confrontation with an angry stranger, it might be best if you drop any need to retaliate by not responding to him and hope your example shows him that there is another way. If enough people refuse to join his fight club, there will be fewer fights.

It's different when anger is directed toward you by an intimate or a boss. Here you can't just walk away—the cost is too great, possibly involving a major life change.

However, because of your ongoing relationship, you have a powerful remedy at hand. For the moment, because of his anger toward you, you may have ceased to exist for him as a human being with virtues and faults. Like a sex object, used only for the gratification of desire, you have become an anger object, a punching bag, on which to vent his rage.

In this situation, you need to remind your attacker of your close, human relationship. This can be done very simply by saying something like, "Your anger hurts" or "Your anger is very painful to me." If he can escape his anger long enough to hear you, this reminder of your vulnerability is likely to give him pause, and you can take that opportunity to start a conversation. "Let's talk about this."

As a prelude to dialogue, be aware of what is going on between you and your attacker. Try to fathom what it is he wants; in other words, what is his unmet demand? It really doesn't matter whether his anger is justified or not. If you can become an observer of the other person's anger and retain your own equanimity, you have the freedom to consider the situation. Where you think that a *mea culpa* is in order, you may want to apologize. Ask yourself if you've failed to meet a legitimate demand that underlies the anger, and can you do so? Are you somehow complicit in the anger? Did you perhaps initiate the outburst by some action like slamming the door? Is it possible there's a misunderstanding? Maybe another's anger is a wake-up call. Are you unaware of something you habitually do that angers other people?

Your most powerful tool in some situations may be what Thich Nhat Hanh calls "compassionate listening." "Sit quietly and listen with only one purpose: to allow the other person to express himself and find relief from his suffering."

The wisdom of this approach has been recognized since ancient Egyptian times:

> *If you are a man who leads,*
> *Listen calmly to the speech of one who pleads;*
> *Don't stop him from purging his body*
> *Of that which he planned to tell.*
> *A man in distress wants to pour out his heart*
> *More than that his case be won.*
>
> —The Instructions of Ptahhotep

Using Humor and Empathy

If the anger of the other person is not too volatile, a show of empathy can sometimes reverse it. When a friend went to pick up some photocopies that were to be ready at 2 P.M., the only clerk was working busily with his back to him. After a while, my friend cleared his throat. The clerk still didn't turn around. When at 2:15 he finally asked, "Can you help me?" the clerk replied testily, "No, you'll have to wait for the other clerk to come back from her break."

"One of those days when everything seems to go wrong?" my friend responded. "I've been there and done that, and it's not fun." Soon afterward, the clerk asked how he could help and handed him his copies.

A marriage counselor needs to draw on empathy when doing mediation with couples who are considering a divorce. During one opening session when the counselor had barely begun explaining the process, the husband, who was hard of hearing, interrupted: "You can't help because you aren't deaf and you can't possibly know what it's like to be deaf."

The counselor agreed. She could not know what it is like to be "deaf," she explained, but she could empathize. She mentioned how isolating it felt when people talked behind her back or talked in front of her like she wasn't there. This simple show of empathy opened up a willingness for him to participate in the dialogue and led to a successful conclusion of the mediation.

Humor can be a powerful tool for deflecting anger, especially when it reveals an absurdity. At one time, I represented a show business personality who had property interests in Tucson. Once when she was flying in on a private jet, she asked me to pick her up so as not to attract attention. When I was heading to the airport, my daughter said she wanted to come along and asked if she could bring a friend who was playing at our house. Without thinking, I said yes. When we pulled up alongside the Gulfstream, the celebrity got out, saw the two children in the backseat, and snarled, "What did you do, sell tickets to my arrival?"

"You found me out," I said. "What if we split the box office?"

She laughed and that was the end of the incident.

Family Feud

When anger arises between members of the same family, the situation is particularly painful. Once entrenched, that anger can become chronic until one person breaks the impasse. Take the case of two sisters, Kate and Jean.

Jean was born six years after Kate, and like many firstborns, Kate resented being dethroned by the interloper. Matters were made worse when the parents had Kate assume some responsibility for baby-sitting, and then later expected her to take her little sister along to tennis lessons and other activities. When Kate got her driver's license, she felt she had become Jean's chauffeur. The resentment toward both her role and her younger sister grew.

After college, Kate moved away and became a teacher. Jean stayed in their hometown and became a successful CPA. Their parents looked to Jean for financial advice, and as they aged, they turned more and more of their money matters over to Jean, until she pretty much controlled everything. When Kate found out, she blew up and demanded that they hire an independent fiduciary. When Jean told her how expensive that would be, Kate proposed that the financial duties be split between the two of them. Jean refused because Kate lived too far away and, furthermore, had never been good at dealing with her own finances.

Kate felt her only recourse was to take legal action. When her attorney told her she had no case, she fired off a letter to Jean, accusing her of stealing their parents' money. Now it was Jean's turn to explode. "Is that what you think of me?" she wrote. "Go to hell, and don't bother calling me because I don't ever want to hear from you again."

It seemed like a permanent rift.

Some years later Jean realized that the stress of her accounting practice and caring for her parents was taking a toll on her health. At her doctor's suggestion, she decided to try meditation, which led to curiosity about Buddhism. When she read how anger acted as a destroyer of happiness, she began thinking about her alienation from her sister. After reading Buddhist teachings on anger, Jean knew she needed to talk to Kate.

Reconciliation began with small steps. Jean called Kate and started with an apology: She said she understood why Kate felt the way she did—Kate had been shut out of the process—and she wanted to make amends. Kate said she would have to think about it.

The next day Kate called back and simply said that she needed to be kept informed about their parents' finances. In the conversation, Jean admitted her arrogance in cutting Kate out of anything having to do with their parents' decisions.

Several calls later Kate admitted that her anger with Jean was a burden she had been carrying, and she was relieved to have an opportunity to heal the rift. The two sisters now consult on all important decisions concerning their parents. Kate has even asked Jean for help managing her own finances, and they visit each other whenever they can.

In this instance, what seemed like an impossible breakdown in an important relationship was healed by Jean's having the courage to reach out and break the impasse. When she did, she discovered that Kate was suffering as well and gradually welcomed the opportunity to mend the situation.

The Case of the Impossible Person

Never wrestle with a hog
The hog gets dirty
You get dirty
But the hog enjoys it.

—American Folk Saying

I n some instances, you may be dealing with a person who is chronically angry. He may be a cynic who is constantly judgmental, because he believes that the world simply does not measure up to his standards. He may even search for occasions to express his angry disapproval as a way of asserting his own superiority. You may want to continue the relationship for various reasons—you have a long history or the person has redeeming qualities that counterbalance the anger. Indeed, what makes him difficult may be what makes him fun and interesting. But if you want to remain friends with this person, you will probably need to accept that his anger is part of the package. When you know him well, you may understand the forces underlying his anger, which may make it easier not to take it personally when his attitude is directed at you.

On the other hand, when you realize that some socially acceptable behaviors are the product of what I think of as an angry personality, you may decide you don't want to have anything to do with such a person. I have recently dropped a couple of old friends in the chronic critic/ cynic category. I realized being with them just makes me unhappy. I don't know whether this is a change in my attitude—I simply don't value these people the way I once did, or I just don't think it's okay to be this way anymore.

Covert anger or passive-aggressive behavior can be difficult to deal with because it's often disguised by words or actions that appear to be normal, even loving. The passive-aggressive person doesn't come out and say that she disagrees with what you ask, she simply doesn't do it. She "forgets" or is chronically late. Establishing limits and consequences is one way to deal with this kind of behavior, for instance, setting a time limit on how long you will wait for a friend who is always late or a penalty for late work. Another is to bring the anger out in the open by asking direct questions: "I feel that you are angry." "Can you help me understand?"

Confronting the passive-aggressive person can be tricky, especially when, as often happens, she is not aware of the anger that underlies her words or actions. It's a good idea to make *your* feelings, and not his or her bad behavior, the subject of the conversation. You might try saying something like, "I heard you repeat what I told you in confidence last night. That really hurt me; please don't do it again."

There's a popular saying, "Don't get mad, get even." But instead of this approach, Shosan Victoria Austin has adopted the motto, "Don't get mad; get effective."

"When I received the precepts, I realized that to use the saying, 'Don't get mad, get even,' was a way of institutionalizing ill will. This approach escalates conflict, and creates wars. For the longest time, I couldn't think of how to handle anger nonviolently without becoming a doormat. When I started going deeper into meditation and yoga, I realized that anger was energy used for unwholesome purposes and that it had an unwholesome effect on the body. I started looking for a peaceful way of using this energy instead."

Austin gives the example of Ellen, a woman whose mean boss was always hypercritical of her. Ellen wanted a promotion and she conceived a strategy that would enable her to rise above the situation. She wrote down everything her boss said about her, and analyzed what concerns were embedded in that hard criticism. When it came time to apply for a higher position, she documented how well she was performing in each area her boss had questioned. She presented that documentation at a higher level and earned a promotion to the same rank as her boss.

Perhaps the worst-case scenario of anger used against us is that in which someone's anger arises not out of his suffering or distress but as a matter of a deliberate strategy. We have probably all been confronted by someone using anger to control or manipulate us. In the business world, in particular, we may run into a superior who believes that anger is a legitimate management tool. In the case of bullying bosses, sometimes simply calling the person on his action is enough to deter him in the future. An art director at a magazine consortium who was the head of his department had a bullying CEO whose means of control was to criticize and belittle him in front of his staff. After one such incident, the friend waited until his boss was alone and then marched into his office and said, "If you ever speak that way to me again, I am out of here." He was not bothered after that.

In many situations, however, an employee cannot afford to do this (you have financial responsibilities and can't leave the job). In such cases, not rising to the bait becomes an essential survival tactic—until you can find another job, that is. Here one can only do as the Dalai Lama does, presumably, in the face of his ongoing conflict with China: "In spite of some very unfortunate circumstances, I usually remain calm, with a settled peace of mind. I think this is very useful. You must not consider tolerance and patience to be signs of weakness. I consider them signs of strength."

✦ *Exercise* RESPONSES TO ANGER

List some examples of someone being angry at you in the past. How would you describe the anger? What did you do? Then write down what you would do now after reading this chapter.

Being faced with a bully or someone wanting to do us harm is an opportunity to develop patience and tolerance—qualities that are essential to our humanity. From this perspective, our antagonist might be viewed as a teacher who can further our progress toward a better life.

If you are willing to risk showing your humanity, even what others might perceive as a sign of weakness, you can de-escalate a spiraling cycle of anger. Acknowledging another person's need is a good opening.

When I have suggested this approach in my workshop, people have said that if they open a dialogue with an antagonist and treat him with kindness, they fear he will become even more demanding of them. I believe this may be a fantasy we use to keep our inherent kindness imprisoned. In any case, why not try doing it as an experiment? The worst outcome is that you may ultimately have to terminate the relationship. On the other hand, you may make (or keep) a friend.

When you no longer view the person who directs anger against you as an adversary but as another human being in distress, you have made a good outcome more likely. It will mean that you have wrestled with a hog and discovered he may not enjoy it after all, and that you have, in any event, benefited from it.

CHAPTER 10

To Be or Not to Be Angry

YOU HAVE A CHOICE

He who controls his rising anger as a skilled driver curbs a speeding chariot, him I call a true charioteer. Others merely hold the reins.

—The Buddha

A woman in Whitefish, Montana, named Laura A. Munson did an extraordinary thing.

When her husband of two decades said to her: "I don't love you anymore. I'm not sure I ever did. I'm moving out. The kids will understand. They'll want me to be happy," she chose not to be angry.

"His words came at me like a speeding fist, a sucker punch, yet somehow in that moment I was able to duck," she wrote in a *New York Times* article. She chose to treat her husband's words like those of a child throwing a tantrum who tries to hit his mother. She ducks and doesn't take the attack personally because it's not about her. She knew her husband well and speculated that this had more to do with his own personal meltdown than with their marriage. Once Munson recovered a bit from the blow and could speak, she managed to say, "I don't buy it."

Doubtless part of the reason she was able to do this was that she had recently committed to "a non-negotiable understanding with herself" that she called "the End of Suffering." She had decided to take responsibility for her own happiness and not allow it to be rooted in things beyond her control. Whether she calls herself a Buddhist or not, she was an exemplar of Buddhist teachings. She kept her equanimity; she chose not to feel humiliated, her pride wounded, to judge or to react with anger. In exemplifying detachment, her "I don't buy it" was the equivalent of the Buddhist monk's "Is that so?"

Not getting angry enabled Munson to see an array of choices. Her hunch was that her husband was in the grip of a profound and troubling midlife crisis and she suggested they take a break—anything but hurting the children and her by leaving.

Being angry or acting out of anger radically narrows our choices for dealing with our lives. When we act out of anger, we are acting nonrationally so, when anger overtakes us, some kind of automatic response kicks in; we focus only on assuaging our anger. This is obvious, but bears repeating as it's usually forgotten when we are in the throes of emotion.

However, if we hold on to our anger—or in Buddhist terms, "harbor ill will"—we may turn it into a perpetual stance that limits our lives on an ongoing basis. We are giving up better choices for ourselves, not only in the moment but in the future. In economics, this is called "lost opportunity cost"—the benefits we could have received had we invested our time, hearts, and minds in something else.

We may each have our own habitual style of solidifying our anger, but generally it will be one of these:

Withdrawal

Revenge

Martyrdom

If someone drops a brick on my foot, anger may rapidly follow my pain. After all, it's reasonable to expect that others not injure me and, in fact, an enraged curse may distract me momentarily. What's important is where I go with that anger. My foot has been injured, and that cannot be undone. But how long I remain angry and the way I deal with my anger will determine its cost to the rest of my life. I can turn my anger to self-pity—"If only this hadn't happened, I could have been happy"—or use it as an excuse to *withdraw* from activity in the short- or longer term.

Or I might focus on *revenge:* "Only when I get even, can I be happy again." In Melville's *Moby Dick*, the ultimate example of this folly, an otherwise capable, rational human being gives his life over to avenging himself against a whale. His single-minded obsession results only in suffering and his eventual death. The unfortunate Captain Ahab perhaps hadn't heard that "living well is the best revenge."

A stance of *martyrdom* can be a devious, indirect way of expressing anger. A person who plays the martyr may be attempting to induce guilt or a sense of obligation in others as a way of manipulating them. "It's okay that you didn't call me when you got there. I was so worried I couldn't sleep." When we choose martyrdom, the story line of our lives becomes, "If I am such a good person, why are people so mean to me?" That view colors everything that happens to us so that even well-intended gestures are interpreted as hostile acts. It's not easy to love a martyr.

✦ *Exercise* LOST OPPORTUNITIES

Can you list opportunities that you lost because you
were focused on the goal of expressing your anger, or
because your anger caused a rift or permanent break in
a relationship?

Anger Causes Bad Karma

In Buddhist thinking, acting out anger carries a residual effect that lasts long after you may have resolved the incident that triggered it. Therefore, it may be helpful to look at anger and choice through the Buddhist concept of *karma*. This word is often misused—for instance, people speak of "parking karma" to mean they're good at finding parking spaces—and the concept with all its different meanings is difficult to understand. The word *karma* literally means "action," but it refers to the workings of the law of cause and effect. As the Dalai Lama defines it, karma "refers to an act we engage in as well as its repercussions."

"When we speak of the karma of killing," he writes in *An Open Heart*, "the act itself would be taking the life of another being. The wider implications of this act, also part of the karma of killing, are the suffering it causes the victim as well as the many who love and are dependent upon that being. The karma of this act also includes certain effects upon the actual killer." No matter how justified the killing was, the karmic effect on the killer may be that having killed once he will need less justification to kill again.

Deepak Chopra says: "'Karma' is both action and the consequence of that action; it is cause and effect simultaneously, because every action generates a force of energy that returns to us in kind. . . . Everyone has heard the expression, 'What you sow is what you reap.' Obviously, if we want to create happiness in our lives, we must learn to sow the seeds of happiness. Therefore, karma implies the action of conscious choice-making."

At any given time, we have an almost unlimited number of choices. We can be ecstatic or depressed or anything in between. We can be aware or unaware. We can undertake our employment with enthusiasm or distaste. However, if we act solely out of anger, the buffet of choice shrinks into a beggar's bowl.

If we are perpetually angry in traffic, we will get in more accidents or near-accidents, thereby generating more opportunity for anger. If we resent our boss and do sloppy work, that may get us fired, which of course, provides more opportunity for anger and resentment. If we insist on always being the dominant party in a relationship, we may wonder why we are not loved more. It goes on and on. We are deliberately, if unconsciously, creating conditions that will deprive us of the things that we want.

We can let anger limit our choices or choose not to be governed by it. If someone or something at work has really made you angry, you may arrive home in that state. At that point, you have a number of choices you might make.

You can tell your wife you want to be left alone while you stew over the day's events, sit in silence during supper, and then withdraw to the television set where you watch the football game by yourself. On the other hand, you might tell your wife that you had a bad day at the office, but now it's wonderful to be in her presence. If she'd like to hear about what happened, you'll be happy to tell her about it. Or you might say, "Gee, I had a lousy day, but I don't want to go into it. Let's go out to dinner and see that movie you were talking about." Although these choices may seem obvious, our habitual patterns may keep us from being aware of them. As always, it's your choice.

At any crossroads, we have many choices and options. We can act creatively. Be who we really are. Go for what we really want. It's important to see our choices as not only one or another—either/or—but a universe of possibilities and strategies.

The Choice is Yours

Not only do we have choices about what we do when we're angry—whether we express it or not, and in what way—but we also can choose not to be angry. The idea that our anger is caused by someone else and is beyond our control is so ingrained that it's hard to avoid saying things like, "Wow, did she make me angry!" We believe that someone else, for reasons of her own, has invaded our turf and that we are innocent victims.

If you become angry, it's a signal that something is wrong. But aside from an asteroid striking you or an unprovoked physical attack that occurs for no reason other than that you were in the wrong place at the wrong time, your anger may be a sign of defensiveness (you have buttons) or a wake-up call to look at what you may have contributed to the situation. Before reading this book, you may have thought choosing not to be angry was beyond your control, but by now it should be evident that in fact you have a lot of choice in the matter.

A friend of mine told me about a time when he was in financial trouble and his wife went on a weekend shopping spree and ran up almost $20,000 in charges. At first he was so enraged that he wanted to divorce her. Then it dawned on him that in his macho way, he hadn't told her about his financial difficulties. When he explained the situation, she immediately offered to return whatever she could. Fortunately, almost everything came from a store that automatically accepted returns. The husband's restraint in not expressing his anger and instead explaining the situation and working with his wife to resolve it resulted in a stronger marriage.

Even if you are free of blame, the choice not to be angry

may be the most beneficial one, as it turned out to be for Laura Munson. For months, Munson endured hostile and unreliable behavior on the part of her husband. Then one day she came home to find him mowing the lawn. He was back. Laura Munson may seem like a saint. But she wasn't a saint; she was smart.

"My husband tried to strike a deal. Blame me for his pain. Unload his feelings of personal disgrace onto me." She didn't buy it and she didn't get angry. And it worked.

✦ NOT SO BLAMELESS

Can you think of an incident, small or large, when you were angry and felt wholly free of responsibility for the situation? It may be a time when you felt righteous indignation and said, "Let me tell you what that SOB did to me." Go back and review it to see if there was anything you might do differently today, given what you now know about the other person's motives, to avoid the problem.

Taking on the Universe

In Chapter 7, we discussed the Buddhist concept that all things in the universe are deeply interconnected in a complex web of cause and effect. This means that everything that has ever happened and is happening anywhere in the universe affects the present moment. Everything, extending from the big bang through the first amoeba dog-paddling across the slime, the dinosaurs, the extinction of the dinosaurs, Columbus (or whoever) discovering America, to what you did yesterday and in the last minute *plus* the butterfly's wings flapping in Brazil, the first drops of dew settling on Mars, and what your adversary's great-great-grandfather did centuries ago are all interacting to create the present moment. So, when we judge the hand we've been dealt as unfair or unacceptable, we are, in effect, taking on the whole universe. The odds of our winning this battle are not good.

When we rail against what has happened, we ignore two important facts. The first is that we can't really know whether what is happening is good for us, and the second is that we can't change it. The issue is not whether we *like* what is happening but whether we understand that *what has happened is not subject to change*.

However, we *can* choose how we react. Just as everything that has ever happened and is happening affects the present moment, so what we choose to think, do, or say *now* also affects the entire universe past, present, and future. If you don't like what just happened, you have the opportunity to change the next installment in the soap opera of your life in grand or subtle ways. Human intelligence gives you the power to react other than by instinct or habit. Intelligence is the power of choice. Anger cripples rational thought and therefore limits your choices. But by using the full power of your intellect and choosing not to act out of anger and habit, you can increase the odds that the events of the future will be more to your liking.

As psychoanalyst Willard Gaylin writes in *Talk Is Not Enough*, "Acknowledging the power we possess in creating our own misery is greatly reassuring. It suggests that we are not passive victims. We are not impotent." The power that we may currently be using to create misery in our lives can be used instead to create our happiness.

CHAPTER 11

Transforming Anger into Compassion

WIELDING THE FLAME OF FURY

Then the raw, neutral energy of anger, the searing flame of fury, the power of the "peaceful" atom can itself become a power tool. It can warm the house, light the darkness, burn away the bonds of ignorance. Compassion can use this fire with fierce effectiveness to destroy the suffering of other beings. Anger usually monopolizes fire, turning it to destructive ends. But . . . we will wield that fire with wisdom and turn it to creative ends.

—Robert Thurman

E ven in the mundane aspects of daily life, anger is most often irrational, based on habitual responses and destructive to our own happiness. We began this book with the tale of "The Cow in the Parking Lot" to illuminate the phenomenon of anger—how it arises in us, how we conspire in its causes and conditions, and how we can gain mastery over the powerful thoughts and emotions that perpetuate unhappiness in ourselves and others.

The next step, transforming anger into compassion, sounds like a giant leap, and it is. It is so contrary to our "normal" way of thinking and our societal norms that it may seem improbable and Pollyanna-ish. So how can such a transformation happen? Where do we begin?

Let us return to the parking lot. Almost universally, when I ask the question, "What is the difference between the cow and the Jeep driver that makes you angry?" the answer is that the man intended to offend, while the cow did not. But, given what we now know about the extent to which our thoughts and actions are conditioned and habitual, and given the general unawareness of most people, can we always assume this?

So the first step in transforming anger is to look at the question of intention. In fact, the Jeep driver, focused only on his goal of grabbing the first available space, may have been totally oblivious to the fact that you were waiting.

Or perhaps, because you approached from the opposite direction, you may not have noticed that he was actually there first. And isn't it a bit of mind reading to think that he intended to harm you? Perhaps his children were sick and he was hurrying to the pharmacy to fill a prescription. Most likely, his notion was that he had as much right to the space as anyone, so you may have pushed his buttons when you blasted your horn. With that aggressive action, you took on some responsibility for the incident. So the line between intentional and unintentional is not as clear as we would like to think. We may believe that we know what another person is thinking, but generally we don't.

The second step on the way to compassion is to count your blessings. Be grateful that the confrontation wasn't worse. He might have rammed your car on the way into the space. Or gotten out of his car and attacked you. Here's another positive: You controlled your anger and didn't act on it further. You were able to maintain your equanimity, which is the greatest blessing we can bestow on ourselves. You didn't pick up that red-hot coal.

It's also a blessing that our encounter with this rude person was brief. We had to deal with him for only a few minutes, whereas he has to live with himself 24/7. We have the option of letting the anger go. He, on the other hand, may continue to seethe because you had the nerve to honk at him.

By this time, it should be easier to take the third step, which is to attempt to view him with compassion. If we decide that we won't express anger because it may bite us back or because we don't like the way it makes us feel, that's a good start. But if we can feel empathy toward those whom we perceive as the cause of our anger, that will strengthen our attitude of compassion toward them and the world in which we live, rather than strengthening a pattern of aggression and an addiction to anger. We can begin by imagining the kind of life our Jeep driver leads. We already know that he is in the grip of his anger, with all the suffering that implies. He is apt to carry this behavior into the rest of his life with predictable results. If his primary mode of expression is anger, then it's probable that nothing comes easily for him.

Or we can view it another way. Is he really so different from you? You can reflect on the fact that, just like you, the Jeep driver wants only to be happy. Perhaps, just like you, he is usually courteous, but at that moment a complex set of conditions led him to succumb to his anger. Perhaps he is at his wit's end because of his sick child. Perhaps he had an abusive, aggressive father who conditioned him to behave this way.

A Zen parable tells of a wise man who returns home to find a thief in his hut. The thief is angry because there is nothing to steal. The wise man, feeling sorry for the thief, offers him his monk's robe. The thief throws down the tattered garment, and storms angrily out into the night. When the wise man goes outside and sits down, the moon is rising over the horizon. "Poor man," he says. "Pity I couldn't have given him the moon."

So now, close your eyes and imagine the scene at the parking lot. The Jeep driver has done his best to be offensive after his act of theft. Then, moving past the anger you felt at first, imagine his life. Following the example of the wise man in the Zen tale, offer him the parking place. Hope that in his torrent of anger, he is able to find some happiness in the event.

Forgiveness

Of course, the loss of a parking spot is small potatoes compared to the larger sufferings that abound in the world. People are killed daily, both intentionally and through the carelessness of others. For their loved ones, such acts may seem unforgivable, yet there are those who are able to forgive. Some relatives of victims of the Oklahoma bombing forgave Timothy McVeigh and did not wish him to be executed.

The Chinese have taken over Tibet. They have killed and tortured many and have destroyed ancient Buddhist monasteries and other artifacts of a unique culture. Despite this ongoing destruction, the Dalai Lama says sutras each day for the well-being of the people who have committed these acts.

The opportunities to turn anger into compassion are, unfortunately, unlimited. Make no mistake. Transforming your anger toward someone who has intentionally trespassed against you and inflicted physical or mental damage is difficult. Nevertheless, we have been given a clear methodology for doing so. In an amazing work from the eighth century, *A Guide to the Bodhisattva Way of Life*, the Indian sage Shantideva lays out a set of precise instructions for why and how we should do this.

Anger, in Buddhist thinking, is not a sin in the Western sense of violating a commandment or a law, but is regarded as an emotional addiction. Anger occurs when irritation, annoyance, disapproval, or something stronger suddenly bursts into an irresistible impulse to respond in a harmful manner to the perceived source of those feelings. "You are not 'expressing your anger,' you have become the involuntary instrument of your anger," says Robert Thurman. "The opposite of anger is love and compassion, the will to help others not to suffer and to be happy." This is similar to what Christian saints and the enlightened beings Buddhism calls *arhats* strive for.

Thurman suggests, however, that it's pushing us mere mortals too far to insist on immediately switching from anger and hate to compassion and love. There is a middle ground of tolerance and forgiveness. So the positive resolve is to cultivate those practices.

In the mental mechanics of anger, there is a moment when we can intervene before the emotion takes over. Says Shantideva:

> *Anger finds its food in the mental discomfort*
> *I feel, faced with the unwanted happening*
> *And the blocking of what I want to happen;*
> *It then explodes and overwhelms me.*

"The key trick," writes Thurman, "is to intervene mentally, verbally, or physically to dissipate the discomfort, to engage the situation energetically, before you explode and lose control to your anger and become its tool." Sometimes you can intervene to change the way things are going. When you see a traffic jam developing on your usual commute, you can get off at an exit ramp and take a different route. When you feel a tug on your purse, you can whirl and demand that the pickpocket give back your wallet. But often you can't, and then you must turn inward and intervene in your mind. If there's no escape from your situation, what's the point of adding anger to your frustration?

There are three methods of working with yourself once anger arises. Thurman calls these methods "tolerant patience," "insightful patience," and "forgiving patience."

The first, "tolerant patience," is what Pema Chödrön describes as "reframing our attitude toward discomfort." If you can sit with your pain—the pain of not retaliating, not returning aggression—you can gradually develop a tolerance and endurance that leads to freedom. "Stay with the underlying heat, the urge to be mean, yell, hit, make somebody wrong," she says in *Don't Bite the Hook*. Examine the addictive urge that makes you want to yell back at somebody, take that drink, or indulge any other addiction, and you will loosen it. If you can sit still with it and not feed the story line—"This is a bad person, I won't let him walk all over me"—you will see that the feeling is fleeting and impermanent and that it will pass. There is scientific evidence, in fact, that the life span of any particular emotion is only one and a half minutes. "After that we have to revive the emotion to get it going again," says Chödrön.

Shantideva advises that we practice with small things in order to be able to cope with larger ones: "Putting up with little cares I train myself to bear with great adversity."

What kind of "little cares"? Shantideva wrote of the bites of insects and snakes, pangs of thirst and hunger, and irritations such as rashes. In our contemporary society, there are the little annoyances that one Tibetan teacher calls "bourgeois suffering." You can train yourself with minor irritations like cell phone rudeness, "computer blues," waiting interminably on the phone with tech support, long lines in the post office, children screaming in a restaurant, and the innumerable other little disturbances of daily life.

"This is not a war against emotion," says Chödrön. "It's opening hearts and minds rather than becoming like a stone." It's not comfortable and requires courage. "Courage is the opposite of cozy," she says. You're going through detox from irritation and anger since anger involves an addiction to adrenaline, and you're cultivating endurance.

The second way of working with your mind is "insightful patience." Here is where you call upon mindfulness and reason to deepen your insight and then to exercise forbearance. Anger always operates within the framework of the concepts we immediately apply to the situation: Someone else is at fault or disagrees with us or is a bad person. A car pauses in the middle of the block and we assume the driver is an inconsiderate idiot talking on his cell phone—until we see that actually he slowed down because a child ran out into the street.

Once when I moved to a new apartment, I was awakened several nights in a row by what sounded like someone dragging furniture across the floor above my bedroom. I went upstairs and testily asked the person who came to the door, "Why are you moving furniture around in the middle of the night?" Behind her, I saw an elderly, heavy woman with a walker beside her bed and understood immediately. Chagrined, I apologized profusely and the next day left a blossoming plant outside her door. She, in turn, made the immense effort to go out with her attendant to get me a box of chocolates. So a friendship began. Similarly, a group of professors were irate that one of their colleagues kept falling asleep in the departmental meetings. They thought he was flipping them off. When he was later diagnosed with narcolepsy, they understood he meant them no disrespect at all.

Even when there is hostile intent behind someone's action, we can take the larger view and understand that, like us, everyone is the product of his conditioning, and every action is determined by a multiplicity of complex forces. In *To Kill A Mockingbird*, Bob Ewell, the town drunk, spits in the face of the attorney, Atticus Finch, who has defended the black man accused of raping Ewell's daughter. Atticus stands there with no hate in his face and just looks at the man, refusing to escalate the violence. Chödrön cites this famous scene, saying, "There is no independent, bad person out there. The whole culture of the South came into that spit, his view of life. How he had been raised." So using insight, you can contemplate the complex reality of any situation and reflect on how it came to be. "When the planes flew into the towers in New York City, was it really just some bad people," she asks, "or a set of complex causes and conditions coming together?"

If somebody spits in our face, she advises, even if you can't feel compassion for him, feel compassion for yourself. At least refrain from being angry. "Do not yield to the addictive urge. Have a little conversation with yourself. 'This person is messed up. This person is basically good but messed up. Why I am getting angry?' If you still become angry, treat it like a temporary relapse like a cloud passing in the sky." And let it go.

Insight allows you to see it's not really your "self" versus your enemy, innocent you versus that bad person. When you realize this, Thurman says, "everything begins to hold a tinge of unreality, fluidity, and you achieve a different level of flexibility of response." Seeing things from many angles enables you to have greater patience.

"Forgiving Patience"

The path of transforming anger into compassion is a long one, through many thickets and false turnings, through setbacks and retracing the path after falling away. Buddhist monks spend lifetimes in study and meditation to attain the enlightenment in which their own egos are subsumed into a feeling of oneness with all other beings. Yet, even while we are fully engaged in this world, there are techniques that help us move toward greater compassion, even for those who have harmed us.

Meditation is a way not only to experience the present but also to investigate the nature of experience and how it comes to be. "The process by which we transform our more instinctual attitude to life, that state of mind which seeks only to satisfy desire and avoid discomforts, is what we mean when we use the word *meditation*," the Dalai Lama writes. "It is the technique by which we diminish the force of old thought habits and develop new ones." As he defines it, meditation is not only zazen, the form of seated meditation in which one attempts to empty the mind. It is also what he calls "analytical meditation," the means by which we familiarize ourselves with new ideas and mental attitudes. "Just as musicians train their hands, athletes their reflexes and techniques, linguists their ear, scholars their perceptions, so we direct our minds and hearts." The whole process of research, of exploring a topic and subjecting it to mental scrutiny, should be thought of as a form of meditation.

So, in a sense, reading this book is a meditation. But simply reading is not enough. The Buddha himself

said, "Don't accept something simply because I say it."
We make his teachings our own by acting on them and
thus empirically testing them—only then do they become
true for us.

When we experiment with patience and tolerance,
we can observe how they create peace of mind in us, make
our environment more harmonious, and engender respect
in others. We can also study compassion by recognizing the
suffering of others and being willing to empathize with
them—to "feel their pain." Yet, it's not easy to truly feel
compassion. One symbol of compassion in Buddhism is a
woman with no arms whose child has fallen into the river.
If we vividly imagine what it's like to be that woman, it's
painful.

It may seem contradictory that to be compassionate
does not mean that we have to sacrifice or suffer ourselves.
But from the Buddhist viewpoint, compassion can only
come from a happy mind. So first, we must have love
and compassion for ourselves. In Buddhism, there is a
concept called *maitri*, a Sanskrit word that is translated as
"unconditional friendship with oneself."

This may be hard for Westerners, with their habits of
self-criticism and constant drive toward self-improvement,
to even stop and consider. *Maitri* means being able to relax
with yourself, to feel at home in your own mind and own

body, to feel one's own essential goodness. That is the seed of happiness. How is it to be achieved? Paradoxically, it comes through not struggling against the pain in our lives. We all face the inevitable pain of growing old, the fear of dying, the loss of our loved ones, and it is natural to want to turn away from that pain. But if we can sit with those pains and bear the tenderness of our own hearts, we can feel compassion for ourselves.

Pema Chödrön observes that often it takes our own sorrow and grief to open us to the pain of others. The loss of her own mother made her feel great compassion for our shared human predicament—we all must die and lose our loved ones to death. When her second marriage fell apart, she found to her surprise that she felt an uncontrived tenderness for other people. "I could look into the eyes of store clerks and car mechanics, beggars and children, and feel our sameness." She tells how a woman whose child died then felt great compassion for all the other women in the world who had lost children. The lesson here is that the tenderness we feel, the softness and vulnerability of our hearts, can open us to love and compassion if we stay with it and don't harden ourselves to avoid the pain we are feeling.

Great compassion doesn't come easily, but we can use "bourgeois suffering" and the small losses that occur in our lives to move in the direction of greater empathy for others. Recently, my pocket was picked. I think I know just when it happened. I was walking on a crowded sidewalk when a young man bumped into me. He got my wallet, which contained about one hundred dollars, my driver's license and credit cards. Since the state of Arizona puts one's social security number on all driver's licenses, I feared the stage was set for identity theft. For the next few days, I faced the irritating tasks of notifying credit card companies and other agencies of the loss and applying for a new license. The feeling that I might have prevented the theft had I been more aware—I saw the thief and felt him touch me—made me even more miserable. But rather than add to my misery by resentment and anger, I decided to practice what I had learned in Buddhism.

I began by mentally thanking the thief for giving me the opportunity to work with my anger as Shantideva advises:

> *Therefore just like treasure appearing in my house*
> *Without any effort on my part to obtain it,*
> *I should be happy to have an enemy*
> *For he assists me in my conduct of Awakening.*

Then, trying to gain insight, I turned my attention to the motives and intentions of the pickpocket. My first thought was that he was probably a drug addict in need of a hit—or perhaps he needed food and shelter because he was mentally ill and couldn't hold a job. I then remembered a story I'd read in the newspaper about a robber who'd comforted the cashier at a convenience store when she became hysterical because he'd held a gun on her. He had needed the twenty dollars he got from the cash register because he hadn't been able to find work to feed his family. If the robber could show compassion, couldn't I do the same? Was I so sure that the pickpocket was my enemy? I imagined him asking me for the money and my giving it to him freely. I remembered the parable "The Giver Should Be Thankful," and thanked my thief again, this time for the opportunity to practice compassion.

As it turned out, my identity was not stolen and none of my credit cards was used. I needed to question my expectation that this would happen and my assumptions about other people.

Once again, I thought of my pickpocket and applied the practice called "Trading Places with Your Enemy." I closed my eyes and tried to walk in the shoes of the person who had offended me. It's cold and I am wearing a coat that isn't very warm and doesn't fit well. I've lost my job and I've stood for hours on the corner where day laborers congregate in hope of getting work and haven't been chosen. I feel miserable at the thought of going home empty-handed to my wife who has worked all day cleaning houses so we can feed the children. "Look at all these rich people on the street," I say to myself. "Any one of them could take care of my problems without really suffering. There's an old well-dressed guy in the crowd with a wallet peeking out of his back pocket. Maybe I can get it."

As I put myself in the man's shoes, I felt that my irritation at losing my wallet was nothing compared with his suffering. Our society had created a situation in which people like me with advantages like being able to go to law school, could prosper, while others couldn't survive. As I shared his pain, I felt compassion and wished I'd been able to offer him the money before he resorted to committing a crime. Poor man, I thought. In other circumstances, I could have been him.

In daily life, just understanding a situation from a broader perspective can enable you to change anger to compassion. Zen priest and Shambhala teacher David Schneider explains it this way: "Thus, for example, becoming a parent, and understanding how the temptation to swat a child arises (not enough sleep, difficult relationship, child unsatisfiable, no quiet, no space, claustrophobia), then understanding how you were swatted, and forgiving your parents for having swatted you. You get it, you understand. You let go. You feel lighter, cleaner.

"And, at the same time, remembering how you were an unsatisfiable child, picky eater, complainer, non-sleeper, and so on, and forgiving the child too, of course. You become more accommodating, and perhaps smarter, about the little teeny places where change might be urged on the child."

In her book *I Know Why the Caged Bird Sings*, Maya Angelou gives another take on becoming your enemy. As a young woman, she decided that she wanted to be the first black conductor on the San Francisco cable cars. Her desire was thwarted by a prejudiced woman clerk who refused to take her application despite the fact that the company was running help-wanted ads. Nevertheless, she persisted and kept applying until her application was accepted.

Later, she concluded: "The miserable encounter had nothing to do with me. The 'me' of me, any more than it had to do with that silly clerk. The incident was a recurring dream, concocted years before by stupid whites and it eternally comes back to haunt us all. The clerk and I were like Hamlet and Laertes in the final scene, where, because of harm done by one ancestor to another, we were bound to duel to the death. Also, because the play must end somewhere, I went further than forgiving the clerk, I accepted her as a fellow victim of the same puppeteer."

With persistence, and without the impediments anger might have created, Angelou got the job.

Compassion for Loved Ones

It is a much more challenging situation when the person causing anger is a loved one. In his book *Anger*, Thich Nhat Hanh has paid special attention to how to heal powerful estrangements between husband and wife. Here he tells a story that illustrates the power of compassionate listening.

I knew a Catholic woman who lives in North America. She suffered very much because she and her husband had a very difficult relationship. They were a well-educated family; they both had doctorate degrees. Yet the husband suffered so much. He was at war with his wife and all of his children. Everyone in the family tried to avoid him, because he was like a bomb ready to explode. His anger was enormous. He believed that his wife and children despised him, because no one wanted to come near him. In fact, his wife did not despise him. His children did not despise him. They were afraid of him. To be close to him was dangerous because he could explode at any time.

One day the wife wanted to kill herself because she could not bear it any longer. She felt she was not able to continue living under these circumstances. But before she committed suicide, she called her friend who was a Buddhist practitioner to let her know what she was planning to do. The Buddhist friend had invited her several times to practice meditation in order to suffer less, but she had always refused. She explained that, as a Catholic, she could not practice or follow Buddhist teachings.

That afternoon, when the Buddhist woman learned that her friend was going to kill herself, she said over the telephone, "You claim to be my friend, and now you are about to die. The only thing I ask of you is to listen to the talk of my teacher, but you refuse. If you are really my friend then please, take a taxi and come listen to the tape, and after that you can die."

When the Catholic woman arrived, her friend let her sit alone in the living room and listen to the dharma talk on restoring communication. During the hour or hour and a half that she listened to the dharma talk, she went through a very deep transformation within herself. She found out many things. She realized that she was partly responsible for her own suffering, and that she had also made her husband suffer a lot. She realized that she had not been able to help him at all. In fact, she had made his suffering heavier and heavier each day because she avoided him. She learned from the dharma talk that in order to help the other person, she should be able to listen deeply with compassion. That was something she had not been able to do in the last five years.

Defusing the Bomb

After listening to the dharma talk, the woman felt very inspired. She wanted to go home and practice deep listening in order to help her husband. But her Buddhist friend said, "No, my friend, you should not do it today because compassionate listening is a very deep teaching. You have to train yourself for at least one or two weeks in order to be able to listen like a Bodhisattva." So the woman invited her Catholic friend to attend a retreat in order to learn more.

There were four hundred and fifty people participating in the retreat—eating, sleeping, and practicing together for six days. During that time, all of us practiced mindful breathing, aware of our in-breath and our out-breath to bring our body and mind together. We practiced mindful walking, investing one hundred percent of ourselves in each step. We practiced mindful breathing, walking, and sitting in order to observe and embrace the suffering within us.

Not only did the participants listen to the dharma talks, but all of us practiced the art of listening to each other, and of using loving speech. We tried to listen deeply in order to understand the suffering of the other person. The Catholic woman practiced very seriously, very deeply, because for her, this was a matter of life or death.

When she returned home after the retreat, she was very calm, and her heart was full of compassion. She really wanted to help her husband to remove the bomb within his heart. She moved very slowly and followed her breathing to keep calm and nourish her compassion. She practiced walking mindfully, and her husband noticed that she was different. Finally, she came close and sat quietly next to him, something that she had never done in the last five years.

She was silent for a long time, maybe ten minutes. Then she gently put her hand on his and said, "My dear, I know you have suffered a lot during the last five years and I am very sorry. I know that I am greatly responsible for your suffering. Not only have I been unable to help you suffer less, but I have made the situation much worse. I have made many mistakes and caused you a great deal of pain. I am extremely sorry. I would like you to give me a chance to begin anew. I want to make you happy, but I have not known how to do it; that is why I have made the situation worse and worse everyday. I don't want to continue like this anymore. So my darling, please help me. I need your help in order to understand you better, in order to love you better. Please tell me what is in your heart. I know you suffer a lot, I must know your suffering so that I will not do the wrong things again and again as in the past. Without you, I cannot do it. I need you to help me so that I will not continue to hurt you. I want only to love you." When she spoke to him like this, he began to cry. He cried like a little boy.

For a long time, his wife had been very sour. She always shouted and her speech had been full of anger, bitterness, blaming, and judging. They had only argued with each other. She had not spoken to him like this in years, with so much love *and tenderness. When she saw her husband crying, she knew that she had a chance. The door of her husband's heart had been closed, but now it was beginning to open again. She knew that she had to be very careful, so she continued her practice of mindful breathing. She said, "Please my dear, please tell me what is in your heart. I want to learn do better so that I won't continue to make mistakes."*

The wife is also an intellectual, she has a Ph.D. degree like her husband, but they suffered because neither of them knew how to practice listening to each other with compassion. But that night she was wonderful, she practiced compassionate listening successfully. It turned out to be a very healing night for both of them. After a few hours together, they were able to reconcile with each other.

While my experience with the pickpocket was more difficult to forgive than the theft of a parking place, this woman's story represents a far more challenging situation. Many of us live with estrangement from parents or siblings, people we love or have once loved who have the power to hurt us deeply. Ultimately, it's far easier to forgive and forget offenses committed against us by people we don't know.

Yet even in situations where our feeling has been frozen for many years, we can change the anger to compassion—both for ourselves and the person from whom we are estranged. The extraordinary healing in the story above was made possible by the woman's motivation. She was so desperate to escape from her suffering that she was ready to kill herself.

When you come together with an estranged person, your most powerful tool for changing things, says Nhat Hanh, is this kind of listening: "You listen not for the purpose of judging, criticizing, or analyzing. You listen only to help the other person to express himself and to find some relief from his suffering. When you share your own suffering, you have the right to say everything in your heart—it is your duty to do so, because the other person has the right to know everything." But you must do so with the condition that you be patient and use kind and loving speech.

If you succeed in sharing your suffering and recognizing the suffering in another, you have opened yourself to the transformative power of love. You have embarked on the road to a spiritual practice and there's a feeling of exaltation that you have probably never experienced before.

The joy of transforming anger into compassion is life-changing. It doesn't matter if you are Christian, Muslim, Jew, or atheist, the door to spirituality has opened in a new way. Transforming anger can make you a better person, no matter what your beliefs. When that happens, I promise, it's an experience you will want to repeat.

CHAPTER 12

Coming to a Conclusion

WHAT HAPPENS WHEN WE GIVE UP ANGER?

With all the knowledge and practice in the world, giving up anger is not easy. It is one of the basic human emotions and it still holds the allure that there's some pleasure or advantage to be derived from it. No one should expect to be free of anger. Despite the benefits you experience from changing your attitudes toward it, overcoming it will most likely require a constant struggle.

Living with anger is like having a lifelong guest in your house. He's been there so long that it hasn't dawned on you that you can evict him. The guest is almost always obnoxious and seems to alienate your family, your neighbors, co-workers, and most everyone else when he intervenes in your affairs. Despite this, you somehow have always considered him a benefit or just a given in your life.

Now it has come to your attention that you can evict him. When you begin to do so, he protests and tries to convince you that you can't live without him—people will take advantage of you in all sorts of ways. If something bad happens in your life, he reappears to tell you that if you hadn't evicted him, it wouldn't have happened. He may convince you to let him back in or he may sneak into the house, and you will have to evict him again and again.

✦

So how do you know when your practice of not being angry is working? What happens when you are successfully applying the process? The good news is that you don't have to reach perfection to benefit from your efforts. As you reduce the amount of anger in your life, you may notice, among other things, that you accomplish what you want more easily. When you dealt with people out of anger, you pushed them away and shut down their basic human generosity. When anger decreases, you allow their Buddha nature to open up. When that happens, people want to help you.

Despite all evidence to the contrary, our society still takes as a given that angry people are powerful and people who are not angry are weaklings. The accomplishments of Mother Teresa, Martin Luther King Jr., Mohandas Gandhi, and Nelson Mandela could only have been achieved by people who were truly powerful.

In the proceedings of the South African Truth and Reconciliation Commission, led by Archbishop Desmond Tutu, the perpetrators of apartheid were invited to come forward to face their victims and the kin of the victims and confess to their crimes enforcing, often brutally, the laws of apartheid. In return, they would receive amnesty for even the most horrible crimes. The commission was based on the concept of *ubuntu*, which the Archbishop explained as follows:

> *Ubuntu* is the essence of being human. *Ubuntu* speaks particularly about the fact that you can't exist as a human being in isolation. It speaks about our interconnectedness. You can't be human all by yourself, and when you have this quality—*ubuntu*— you are known for your generosity.
>
> We think of ourselves far too frequently as just individuals, separated from one another, whereas you are connected and what you do affects the whole world. When you do well, it spreads out; it is for the whole of humanity.

As the proceedings progressed, it became clear that when many of the victims and the survivors heard the people who had killed, tortured, and maimed their loved ones confess and express contrition, their need for revenge began to decrease and forgiveness became possible. What had occurred is that they no longer felt powerless. Also, their own (undeserved) guilt was alleviated. A child who had watched his parents being killed said that for the first time, he really understood that he was not responsible for their death and that he could not have stopped it. Thus, the sharing of humanity between the perpetrator and his victims allowed for the dissipation of anger and guilt.

Despite giving workshops and writing a book on transforming anger, I still get angry. From time to time, I get a reminder from an unexpected source that brings me back to my intention. Recently when I was in a hardware store getting a bunch of supplies for remodeling my home, I could feel my blood pressure going up as the salesperson continued to misunderstand what I wanted. I thought, "Anger is the only thing that will get through to him." Just as this thought was making its way toward action, I heard a voice from behind me say, "You know, I gave up anger about ten years ago." I turned and saw a forty-something employee talking to a twenty-something employee no more than three feet behind me. The older employee continued, "I finally figured out that it caused more problems than it solved." I got the message and used patience instead.

When I related this to my teacher, Patrick Hawk, his explanation pointed the way forward. "Once you give up your attachments to things like anger," he said, "you become more aware, and it opens the door to things that you might have missed out on before. It may feel miraculous. But it isn't. It's just what's there." What I understood him to mean wasn't about the recent incident, it was that the universe hands out things we don't like, but it's also a source of goodness and joy. When we are unaware, the bad may force its way into consciousness, and the good is obscured by our conditioning, judgments, and beliefs.

Giving up anger requires attention and resolve. A classic Native American tale of our ongoing battle goes like this:

One evening an old Cherokee told his grandson about a battle that goes on inside all people. He said, "My son, the battle is between two 'wolves' inside us all.

"One is Evil. It is anger, envy, jealousy, sorrow, regret, greed, arrogance, self-pity, guilt, resentment, inferiority, lies, false pride, superiority, and ego.

"The other is Good. It is joy, peace, love, hope, serenity, humility, kindness, benevolence, empathy, generosity, truth, compassion, and faith."

The grandson thought about it for a minute and then asked his grandfather: "Which wolf wins?"

The old Cherokee simply replied, "The one you feed."

I purposely called this final chapter "Coming to a Conclusion" because the conclusion of this book is for you to make. Do you want to continue as you are, or do you want to change the way anger influences your life? The choice is up to you.

By this point in your reading you should know that your permit for carrying concealed anger has been revoked. In its place there is a card "In Case of Anger, Read This" on page 193. If you want, cut it out along the dotted lines and carry it in your wallet for the next anger attack, which is almost certainly on the way. When you do become angry, take a look at the card and ask yourself, "Do I really want to be angry?" If your answer is "Yes," then ask yourself, "Why?" If your answer is that the other person deserves your anger, then ask yourself if *you* deserve your anger.

If your anger still remains, you may find it helpful to reread this book, which may have a different meaning after your conscious efforts to apply its teachings. Hopefully, you will have experienced at least some benefit from letting go of anger so that you will want to continue on this path. As with many things in life, we must begin over and over again.

Almost everything you need to know from this book can be summarized in a single, powerful sutra from the Dhammapada:

Mind is the forerunner of all actions.
All deeds are led by mind, created by mind.
If one speaks or acts with a corrupt mind,
*   suffering follows,*
As the wheel follows the hoof of the ox pulling a cart.
Mind is the forerunner of all actions.
All deeds are led by mind, created by mind.
If one speaks or acts with a serene mind,
*   happiness follows,*
As surely as one's shadow.

He abused me, mistreated me, defeated me, robbed me.
Harboring such thoughts keeps hatred alive.
Releasing such thoughts banishes hatred for all time.
Animosity does not eradicate animosity.
Only by loving-kindness is animosity dissolved.
This law is ancient and eternal.

Cut out this card along the dotted lines,
and carry it with you in your wallet.
(See page 190.) You may want to make
several copies or laminate it.

IN CASE OF **ANGER,** READ THIS

Anger is a destructive
emotion.

— • —

The first person damaged
by my anger is me.

— • —

Action taken when I am
angry is going to be irrational
and probably stupid.

— • —

I can, if I choose,
reduce the amount of
anger in my life.

— • —

As I reduce anger, I will be
happier and more effective.

Further Reading

This book draws on many Buddhist books and sources, among them the following:

Anderson, Reb. *Being Upright: Zen Meditation and the Bodhisattva Precepts.* Berkeley, Calif.: Rodmell Press, 2001.

Chödrön, Pema. *Don't Bite the Hook: Finding Freedom from Anger, Resentment, and Other Destructive Emotions.* Boston: Shambhala Audio, 2007.

———. "The Natural Warmth of the Heart." *Shambhala Sun.* November 2009.

Chödron, Thubten. *Working with Anger.* Ithaca, N.Y.: Snow Lion Publications, 2001.

Gyatso, Tenzin (His Holiness, The Fourteenth Dalai Lama). *An Open Heart*. New York: Little, Brown, 2001.

———. *Healing Anger: The Power of Patience from a Buddhist Perspective*. Translated by Geshe Thupten Jinpa. Ithaca, N.Y.: Snow Lion Publications, 1997.

Gyatso, Tenzin and Howard C. Cutler, M.D. *The Art of Happiness*. New York: Riverhead Books, 1998.

Kaviratna, Harischandra, trans. *Dhammapada (The Way of Truth): Wisdom of the Buddha*. Pasadena, Calif.: Theosophical University Press, 1980.

Kornfield, Jack. *After the Ecstasy, the Laundry: How the Heart Grows Wise on the Spiritual Path*. New York: Bantam Books, 2001.

Mipham, Sakyong. *Ruling Your World: Ancient Strategies for Modern Life*. New York: Broadway Books, 2005.

Nhat Hanh, Thich. *Anger: Wisdom for Cooling the Flames*. New York: Riverhead Books, 2001.

Reps, Paul and Ngoyen Sensak. *Zen Flesh, Zen Bones*. North Clarendon, Vt.: Tuttle Publishing, 1985.

Suzuki, Shunryu. *Zen Mind, Beginner's Mind*. New York & Tokyo: Weatherhill, 1986.

Tanahashi, Kazuaki. *A Flock of Fools: Ancient Buddhist Tales of Wisdom and Laughter from the One Hundred Parable Sutra*. Translated by Peter Levitt. New York: Grove Press, 2004.

———. *Essential Zen*. Edited by Tensho David Schneider. New York: HarperCollins, 1995.

Tarrant, John. *The Light Inside the Dark: Zen, Soul, and the Spiritual Life*. New York: HarperCollins, 1998.

Thurman, Robert A. F. *Anger: The Seven Deadly Sins*. New York: Oxford University Press, 2005.

———. *Essential Tibetan Buddhism*. San Francisco: HarperCollins, 1999.

Acknowledgments

Susan Edmiston would like to thank Tensho David Schneider for introducing her to Buddhism, Shosan Victoria Austin for her ongoing inspiration and help with this book, and the teachers and sangha of the San Francisco Zen Center, whose wisdom, serenity and loving-kindness emanate throughout this world.

Many thanks to friend and agent Andree Abecassis for her valuable advice during the evolution of this book and to agent Laurie Harper for her advice on the contract. Great gratitude goes to Ruth Sullivan for embodying grace and patience in the editing process and to Peter Workman for believing in this book.

31901046686905

Len Scheff would like to thank John Tarrant and Father Patrick Hawk Roshi.